# Praise for *Why Not*

"Sharing directly from the heart of his own experience, Eric has laid down large footprints that you may triumphantly follow to the pinnacle of your own divine, creative purpose."

— Michael Beckwith, D.D. and author,
*Forty-Day Mind Fast–Soul Feast*
and *A Manifesto of Peace*

"Read this book carefully; there are jewels of wisdom on every page. The lessons that Eric passes along from his father on failure and frustration are worth their weight in gold."

— Bob Proctor, speaker and author of
the bestselling *You Were Born Rich*

"*Why Not* calls us back to our own authentic selves, and the source of all our genuine creativity and capacity for choice. Eric DelaBarre locates that authentic self in the capacity to love beyond ignorance and fear, and in the courage to live life in its terms. This charming book, so beautifully crafted in intention and language, is a precious work in the new civilization in which we all hope."

— Brother Wayne Teasdale, monk and author of
*A Monk in the World* and *The Mystic Heart*

"*Why Not* will open your mind and touch your heart. Eric DelaBarre is an unstoppable inspiration!"

— Cynthia Kersey, speaker and
author of *Unstoppable*

"*Why Not* is an astute and rejuvenating affirmation. A positive tool for awakening *your* life journey."

— Mr. Robin Lopez, Operations Manager,
Pepsi-Cola Company

# WHY NOT

## $\int$tart living your life today

### ERIC DELABARRE

 Seven Publishing • Santa Monica, California

SEVEN PUBLISHING
P.O. Box 1123
Santa Monica, CA 90406-1123
seven@sevenpublishing.com
www.sevenpublishing.com
877 595-6996

WHY NOT © 2003 by Eric DelaBarre

Seven Publishing First Edition 2003
Manufactured in the United States of America

LCCN 2002094062
ISBN 0-9723578-7-4

*Interior design & typesetting by Sara Patton Book
Production Services (800) 433-4804
Cover design by Kathi Dunn of Dunn+Associates
www.dunn-design.com
Illustrations by Garret S. DelaBarre
Printing by Central Plains Book manufacturing
www.centralplainsbook.com
Author photograph by Bader Howar www.baderphoto.com
Proofing by Tracey Creech
Sunglasses by Oakley U.S.A.
Inspiration by GOD*

# $\mathcal{C}$ontents

INTRODUCTION ........................................................... I

CHAPTER 1      Living in the Dream Stream .................. 12
*Are you ready to dive in?*

CHAPTER 2      The Other P.M.S. ............................ 23
*Your positive mental state.*

CHAPTER 3      Don't Miss Your Conscious Bliss .......... 30
*The art of waking up.*

CHAPTER 4      The Moment of "Ah ha" ....................... 41
*The day I woke up and said, "Why not?"*

CHAPTER 5      The Status Quo Woes .......................... 48
*Breaking free with passion.*

CHAPTER 6      Stress .......................................... 60
*Is it running your life?*

CHAPTER 7      Life Is But a Dream ............................ 69
*If there's no wind, row your own boat.*

CHAPTER 8      Practical People ............................... 75
*– get practical lives.*

CHAPTER 9      "I'm Not Creative" ............................ 81
*An exercise in trust.*

CHAPTER 10      Lights! Ideas! Action! ....................... 89
*Your life is waiting!*

CHAPTER 11      Put Another Log On the Fire ............... 96
*What are you waiting for?*

CHAPTER 12      New Year's Resolutions ...................... 101
*Change is NOW!*

CHAPTER 13    Yesterday ................................. 106
              *Leave your troubles, come on, be happy!*

CHAPTER 14    I'm So #@$*% Mad! ........................ III
              *Stopping anger before it starts.*

CHAPTER 15    What Goes Around Comes Around ..... 116
              *The gifts of giving.*

CHAPTER 16    Risk ..................................... 123
              *A four-letter word?*

CHAPTER 17    Success Finds a Way ...................... 127
              *Can it find you?*

CHAPTER 18    Most of All .............................. 144
              *Being proud of yourself.*


Works Cited/Permissions ............................... 153
Bibliography/Research ................................. 154

*Dedicated to love and compassion*

### Disclaimer from the Author's Heart

Although everything you're about to read is from my true, authentic self, an occasional opinion might appear somewhere within this book. Going a bit further, you might also discover an opinion of an opinion. You see, through my personal development and continued unfolding to the man I am becoming, I may not be aware of those opinions. Virtually every time I go back through the material for a rewrite, there is something new and exciting to share. When I discover these new and exciting things, my awareness level is raised and it's at this point I recognize some opinions that slipped through the radar the last time around. Much in the way life is described as a "journey and not a destination," writers never really "arrive" with their work. We merely find a place to stop. Based on that knowing, what you're about to read is from my heart, right here, right now. I look forward to the unknown, based on what I know today.

### Disclaimer from the Lawyer's Heart

*Why Not* is designed from one man's heart to the hearts of those who choose to read it. It is also designed to educate and entertain. The author and Seven Publishing shall have neither liability nor responsibility to any person or entity with respect to any loss or damage, caused, or alleged to have caused, directly or indirectly, by the information contained in this book. If you do not wish to be bound by the above, you may return the unused book to the publisher for a refund.

# FOREWORD

Are you familiar with the term *bioluminescence*? Even since college, I've loved this word and recently have found a correlation that was perfect for my foreword. Bioluminescence is the emission of light from living organisms by way of a chemical reaction and movement. Bioluminescence is primarily a marine phenomenon which is predominantly found in the mesopelagic zone—a depth range from 200 to 1,000 meters. Approximately 90% of all life (fish, shrimp, squid, and gelatinous zooplankton) in this zone are bioluminescent. Scientists aren't sure why, but it seems bioluminescence is essentially absent—with a few exceptions—in fresh water. On land it is most commonly seen in some earthworms, centipedes, certain kinds of fungi or in the few families of luminous insects such as the fire fly or lightning bug.

If we open our minds, we can see how much we have in common with these bioluminescent organisms. Have you ever heard someone say, "You are absolutely glowing today"? Usually when someone says this, you're either having a really good day, you're pregnant, or you might've been in love. In reality, what's occurring is a simple chemical reaction within your body. This chemical reaction produces a feeling of joy and happiness through the release of serotonin and dopamine. In short, as living and moving organisms, we have the ability to create light in the darkest of times. Michael Beckwith, D.D., Founder and Spiritual Director of the Agape International

Spiritual Center, describes this feeling going on inside of us as our "vibratory frequency." For the longest time I had been trying to find a human correlation to bioluminescence and through him, I found it. Basically, this vibratory frequency defines our position in life, moment by moment. "There are no days in life so memorable as those which vibrated to some stroke of the imagination." – Ralph Waldo Emerson (1803–1882). As we continue to unfold into the amazing, creative, passionate, joyous and blissful people that we actually are, we become more conscious of the power of our thoughts, words and actions. In essence, we are what we think. The burning question remains: How are you thinking? What are you concentrating on?

Vibratory frequency is essential to every day living and it can go either direction: positive or negative. When we become angry, our vibratory frequency causes all sorts of internal damage which is commonly referred to as stress. Prolonged exposure to stress can lead to heart disease, high blood pressure and other aliments. The ultimate frequency to achieve in life is one filled with love and compassion. We have the ability to light up our lives and the lives of others by operating at this vibratory level. Are you choosing your vibration in life? Are you choosing love over anger, or have you been snagged by the circumstances, appearances and perceptions of your life? Close your eyes and think about a time in your life that you were the happiest. This could be your wedding day, your child's graduation, or any other day filled with love. This feeling tonality can also be achieved when you hear your favorite song. Your heart space is filling with love and fondness. When we move into this type of heart space, we become filled with light. Essentially, we become bioluminescent. By way of a feeling tone, we are in love and you know what they say: "Love conquers all."

This phenomenon has nothing to do with motivation, either. As soon as this chemical reaction occurs within our bodies, science takes over. The question remains, would you like to feel this way every day of your life? Filled with love and compassion? Some think this feeling tone is only reserved for the vacations in life. No, no, no. The key is to bring your "vacation mentality" to your every day life by becoming conscious of your vibratory frequency. A feeling tone with a firm foundation of love is yours for the taking. If you want it, all you have to do is claim it. You see, by claiming this vibration, we are no longer living our lives, we are living our love. When we do that, nothing else really matters. Are you ready for that kind of happiness in life? Are you ready to dive into a life you often only dream about? Change your vibration so that you can feel the seat of your soul moving with love and your possibilities will become endless. Everything begins and ends with love. Everything begins and ends with you!

"There are those who look at things the way they are, and ask why . . . I dream of things that never were, and ask *why not?*"

– Robert F. Kennedy (1925–1968)

# INTRODUCTION

Flashing like a road sign, the blinking cursor was waiting. How do I begin? What's my first line? What's my first chapter going to be? For days I stared at an empty screen wondering how—and more importantly, where—the beginning should begin. I remember thinking, "Oh God, I'm lost and I haven't even started." My mind began to swirl with thoughts of doubt. "You've never written a book before! What makes you think you can do it now? Nobody will ever read it." Over and over like lines in a song, these thoughts of doubt went on and on. "A pessimist sees the difficulty in every opportunity; an optimist sees the opportunity in every difficulty." – Winston Churchill (1874–1965).

I had never experienced writer's block before, so I couldn't understand why it was happening now. I knew it wasn't a matter of coming up with something to say, because I had eight years' worth of sketch books filled with thoughts, inspirations, and dreams. Truth be told, I was snagged by my own thoughts of lack and limitation. I felt like a fraud because I was trying to write a book about conquering the very thing I was suffering from: fear of the unknown. How could I write a book about capturing your heart's desire and the courage to follow it through when I was blinded by fear? Was it because I was about to expose my innermost thoughts and desires for everyone to read? Was it because I was doing something that I had never done before?

Have you ever felt stuck like this? So stuck that you weren't sure what to do? I've always believed writer's block is caused by uncertainty. The writer isn't sure what to say. It's simple, really. All we have to do is find a direction and the block is lifted. This philosophy can be applied to our everyday lives when we feel stuck. All we have to do is find a direction and make a decision. After the decision, all you have to do is trust in your heart. When you do that, nothing else matters. You're answering the call of your inner most desire and *that's* what life is really about. It's not about the big house and fancy car, I assure you. We're talking about your heart and giving and receiving love. If you're searching for reassurance, take a look in the mirror because *you* are everything *you* need.

A month later, the title of the book finally came to me. It was this very title that would push me through the darkness of fear, doubt, and worry and into the light of action and confidence. *"Why not* write the book?" The words played over and over in my head, quelling my fears because this was the answer. The answer was the whole philosophy behind the phrase "why not." *Why not* write this book? *Why not* follow a dream of expression? Would my ego take a blow if nobody liked it? Since the ego wasn't involved with the inception of the idea, the answer would be no. Ego is a waste of time, so let's start right now by kicking it to the curb where it belongs.

When I thought about writing the book in terms of *why not,* my fear of writing the book was overpowered by the thought of never giving it a try. I knew if I didn't at least try, I would forever regret it. Since I choose to live my life without any regrets—past, present, or future, I embraced the desire and dove in, despite the fear. How can you accomplish this for yourself? The key is to stop dreaming about your life and start living it. Do what you dream, not what you fear! Put your ideas into action. If you embrace your dreams, fear will fall into the nothingness from where it once came. Some say you have nothing to fear but fear itself. I disagree. Being afraid of fear is putting your attention on the wrong thing: fear. The secret is to put your attention on what you desire. The secret is to put your attention on your "intention." Wake up to the possibilities in your life by focusing on your dreams! When you do this, you won't wait around for opportunity to knock. You will have already kicked the door wide open. Live your life wide open by focusing on your dreams. "Some of us have great runways already built for us. If you have one, take off! But if you don't have one, realize it is your responsibility to grab a shovel and build one for yourself—and for those who will follow after you." – Amelia Earhart (1897–1937).

Awakening is merely a starting point. Knowing you'll suffer regret if you don't do something is a gift. A lot of people want to forget about their dreams because they are afraid of what has happened, what might happen, or what will happen in their lives. In order to live the life you dream about, you have to let go of fear associated with giving it a shot. You have to let go of doubt. You have to let go of worry. You have to let go of any thoughts of lack and embrace the "right now" of your dreams. When I asked myself whether or not it was worth facing my fears about writing this book, I answered with a resounding yes and began to write. The word "yes" is a great tool for dream realization. Are you using it on a daily basis?

In the quiet moments of our lives, we often dream about a life that seems so far away. That's a misconception grown out of fear, doubt and worry. If you can imagine it, you can obtain it. I remember when I was in college and I used to think about making movies. It seemed impossible. As you'll later read, I've proven that making a movie and then watching it on HBO isn't impossible. Life is only impossible when we give away the power of possibilities by living in fear, doubt and worry. Writing this book has been a roller coaster ride of emotions that rivals any amusement park ride in the world. I've learned more about myself throughout this journey because I'm doing something I've never done before. If you're looking to feel alive, embrace the unknown of your life. Embrace something you fear. I've never written a book before, but why should that stop me? We have to start somewhere, right? *Why not* start right here? *Why not* start right now?

External validation is a waste of time and emotion. The only validation you need is the knowing you can do whatever you want as long as you follow your heart. Know that you are qualified to be whatever you want to be. Don't wait for someone's permission to do something in your life. Your dreams are your dreams and the only person you need to answer to is your authentic self. Is your dream authentic to your heart? Yes? Then waiting for someone to qualify you is merely *you* keeping *you* in a comfort zone. Comfort zones are a waste of time. Waiting for someone to be proud of you or what you're doing is also a waste of time. I'm proud of myself for writing this book. I'm proud of myself because I'm doing something I've always dreamed about. This book started close to fifteen years ago, but it's finally here, regardless of what someone else might've said about my doing it. The only validation I need is within my heart. As Mae West (1892–1980) once said, "He who hesitates is a damned fool." This sounds harsh, but it's true. Listen to the little cartoon cricket and sing, "I'm no fool, no sirree."

Through the execution of my own expression, I've become more of who I am. Isn't that what life is all about—moving in the direction of your dreams? My dreams are centered on artistic expression, and this is my latest. One of the most amazing things I've learned during this process is to be careful about how I think and dream. We must be careful of how we dream, because our dreams just might come true. Are you ready for that? Are you ready to be more of who you already are? Are you ready for everything you've ever dreamed of? You see, your dreams are waiting for you to break free from the confines of society and other peoples' perception of you, not to mention your own perception of yourself. Your dreams are waiting for you to claim them. Your own personal greatness is waiting for you to claim it. Are you ready to claim it? Zig Ziglar, one of the great motivational speakers of our time once said, "What you get by reaching your goals is not nearly as important as what you become by reaching them." You can find more information on Mr. Ziglar at www.zigziglar.com.

When we move in the direction of our dreams, two things happen. The first, usually the one that makes us cry, is that we encounter the dark clouds of uncertainty and self-negativity. I experienced this when I set out to write the book. The second, which is usually the one that makes us smile, is that we realize we're doing what we set out to do. This is very powerful and an exciting feeling to have because this is where the love resides. When you embrace something that has the capacity to move your heart, nothing else matters. If you feel it in your heart, love will carry you through. When you're led by love, nothing can stop you. The secret is to feel. Feel your life and claim it every day.

When I began putting my dreams down on paper in 1988, I confided in a friend that I wanted to write a book one day. He asked, "How do you come up with all these things you want to do with your life?" I wasn't sure what he meant by this. He thought I wanted to be a filmmaker. I do. I accomplished that, as you'll soon read, but I've always wanted to write a book, produce a CD, and do just about a million other things connected with the expression of my heart. I soon discovered that my friend wasn't sure what *he* was going to do after college. He didn't have anything pulling him because all he had done so far in his life was play college football. He was finally coming to the realization that he was only a "college player" because of his size. He wasn't big enough for the NFL, and he often felt like there was nothing left to do but move back home and work for his dad. Have you ever felt this type of retreat in your life? Next time you feel it, don't give in to it. Never fold up your tent and settle for a comfort zone. You never know what might happen, or what will happen, if you give your dreams a shot. Capture your dreams on a daily basis. If you won't, who will?

I thought about my friend's question for a long time until the answer finally came. It was during college, and I was sitting on the patio of my apartment on a rainy Tuesday afternoon when I realized, "I just do it." I make a conscious decision to go after what I feel in my heart. It's not like some lightning bolt of inspiration, either. Sure, lightning bolts can happen in our lives, but most of the time, our dreams are born in the quiet moments of our lives. For me, the desire to write a book happened while I was writing in my journal during a camping trip to Half Dome in Yosemite National Park. Once this idea came into my consciousness, I had a choice to either act on it, or ignore it. Most people choose to ignore ideas because they think of them as being impossible. Remember, you can't spell impossible without the word possible. I choose to act upon my dreams and make them become my reality. *Why not?* Are you having trouble feeling your hearts desire? Not sure what your calling is? Are you listening to the love in your heart, or are you listening to the fears in your head? Fear will cause you to ignore your dreams. Fight for the rights of your dreams. Don't let fear define your reality.

If you feel as if your life is lacking passion, your life might be lacking practice. Passion is born out of practice. When you trust in your desire, you are allowing yourself to become passionate about the desire. The longer you trust in the desire, the sooner you'll become passionate about it. For example, if you have a desire to learn how to scuba dive, answer the desire with action and become certified in the sport. Now, what usually happens through practice is you'll discover whether or not you love scuba diving. If you indeed like it, you'll want to do it more often. The more you do it, the more passionate you'll become about it. It's a cyclical occurrence. Before you know it, you'll own a dive shop in Hawaii living a dream. Not a bad life if it's something you're passionate about. I guess what I'm trying to say is, you can't expect to sit down at a piano one day, play "Chopsticks," and suddenly have the passion to become a concert pianist. It doesn't happen that way. The more you play, the more passionate you become, if it's your calling. The only way to answer the call is through practice. The only way to find a calling is to listen to what pulls your heart. Everyone has a calling. Ask yourself the question, "What do I dream about?" When you answer that, the equation is no longer an equation. It's a solution which is born out of love and executed through practice.

Through media exploitation, peer pressure, and other external societal circumstances, we've become anesthetized to the good that is waiting for us to claim in our lives. Remaining in the confines of "society" is only a crime against yourself. It's time to step out of your comfort zone and start claiming your life on a daily basis. The funny thing about comfort zone living is that the life usually lacks any sort of comfort whatsoever. After all, isn't the comfort zone keeping you in the status quo of your life and away from your true desires? What's so comfortable about that? Just because it's familiar doesn't mean it's comfortable. Become an individual and know that miracles are waiting to happen in your life. Remember what Albert Einstein (1879–1955) had to say about miracles and life: "There are two ways to live your life. One is as though nothing is a miracle. The other is as though everything is a miracle." Some of you might ask, "What makes me so special that miracles are waiting for me?" Miracles aren't waiting for you, they *are* you. *You* are the miracles you seek. Are you willing to smile during your struggles for success? Are you willing to accept and use your failures gracefully? Are you willing to accept that you have to start somewhere? Can you admit that "somewhere" is nowhere near the top? Are you willing to accept that you're unique in every way? Everybody is different from everybody else. We're different shapes, sizes, and colors: we're endowed with different attitudes; we possess different dreams and different bank accounts; basically, we're different in every way. Knowing this, it's time to stop comparing yourself to the world. Why compare yourself to the next person? You *are* you, and that in itself is exciting enough to drive you toward your goal. I love who I am. I wouldn't want to be anyone else, because that would make me them and not me. Emulation can be a great thing, but if you lose sight of who you are, how great can it be?

I can hear the debates percolating already. The "next guy" has an easier climb than I do. She's got more money, or he knows all the right people. We have a million excuses for why our dreams *won't* come true. We're looking for any reason to justify our failures before we've even had the chance to fail. When we look for a reason why something *won't* happen, chances are it *won't*. Children, careers, money, parents, support groups, skin color, sexual preferences, too poor, too tall, too short, too old, too young, too ugly, too many kids, too pretty—you name it and we'll find a reason why our own personal success is unattainable. Steer clear from these excuses and focus on the good waiting to happen in your life. Focus on the reasons why you're going to succeed, not the excuses why you won't. Is your attention on your intention? In order for all of this good to come forth, you have to adopt an unstoppable knowing about yourself. Not a belief, but a *knowing*. When we believe something, we're still trying to convince ourselves. When we know something, we no longer have to believe in it. In short, we just know it to be true. You don't *believe* that water is wet, do you? That ice is cold? No. These are things you know. Apply that same philosophy to yourself and your life. Know that you're unstoppable! Know that you're creative! Know that you are special! Know that everything you dream is a possibility! Simply *know* that your life is an amazing thing! Your life is the gift that keeps on giving. Never be the force that defeats your own drive. *Why not* be the force that powers you through to accomplish whatever you seek? Stop looking for external situations or circumstances to empower you. Everything you need is already inside of you.

We're going to discuss how to be "awake" during your life's journey and how to halt self-scrutiny before it has a chance to begin. Did you know some people are so subconsciously frightened of becoming what they dream of that they'll do anything to sabotage themselves? Playing small or self-defeating actions serve nobody. Each and every one of us deserves greatness. Know that you are powerful and extraordinary. I love who I am and where I am going. Do you know how it feels to say something like that? Have you said it today? Did you say it yesterday? How about we say it right now? "I love who I am and I love where I'm going." Success is a process much like life. Our personal success is a journey, not a destination. We've heard it before, but maybe we need to *listen* this time and actually *hear* it.

I know I've made this mistake hundreds of times: "When I get the promotion," "When I meet the right girl," "When I buy a house," "When I get a new car," "When I get a raise" (which reveals one of our biggest hang-ups about success: money), then everything will fall into place. Who are we kidding? My procrastination took this form: "I'll write my book 'when' I achieve greatness as a film director." You see, I used to think this would legitimize me in the eyes of the publishing world. The two are not related. Time waits for no one. This "when" philosophy is a trap because "when" is right now. Don't base your happiness on something other than right now. Now is the time for happiness. Now is the time for joy. Now is the time for bliss. Rich man, poor man, happiness is a state of mind. What state do you want to live in? How happy do you want to be? Everything is up to you. Are you ready?

At the end of each chapter you will find an exercise section to help you put what you've read into action. Make these exercises a daily practice and trust through a feeling tone of love and acceptance. Simply put, you need to trust in the path you've chosen. Trust in your desire to ask the tough questions about your life. Trust in the vision you are creating for change. Trust in yourself to withstand any thoughts of fear or limitation that someone might discover you're reading a personal growth or motivational book. For some reason, it is more acceptable read a sports or fashion magazine than it is to read something that might actually make a difference in your life. Stop worrying about what other people might think of you and start capturing your dreams by diving into your life. Simply trust in who you are, and more importantly, trust in who you are becoming.

*Important:* Please understand that the material you're about to read does not subscribe to a "fast food" mentality.

There are no "add-water" fixes when our personal development is concerned. You will soon discover the actual reading won't take that much time at all. What will take time is the implementation and commitment to what you've read. I suggest a chapter every Sunday evening. This will enable you time for contemplation, digestion and discernment throughout your week. If Sunday doesn't serve you best, find a schedule that works best for you, but please stick to it. Your commitment to yourself starts right here. Are you ready?

# 1

# $\mathcal{L}$iving in the Dream Stream

## *Are you ready to dive in?*

Living in the dream stream simply means putting yourself into the game of your choice. Are you a firefighter? Are you an executive on Wall Street? Are you a teacher? Whatever you choose, you can't expect great things to happen if you're sitting on the sidelines of life. Put yourself in the game! You're the coach of this team, so get in there and mix it up. Are you waiting for external validation? Are you waiting for an invitation? Guess what, you already have one—your heart is your invitation. All you have to do now is follow it and you'll be rewarded with all that you desire. "The future belongs to those who believe in the beauty of their dreams." – Eleanor Roosevelt (1884–1962).

Before we get into the stream of our dreams, we have to drop some weight. I'm not talking about trimming your waistline, I'm referring to the stuff that pulls you down and clouds your focus during the pursuit of your dreams. Basically, it is anything that stops you from becoming who you really are. Associating with negative people, indulging in time-sinking activities like video games, watching massive amounts of television, overindulgence of alcohol, drugs, being a workaholic, revisiting past experiences, or dwelling on poor opinions of yourself, are just some of the things that might distract your focus. These activities are different, but the one thing they all have in common is *you*. *You* have the power to "allow" or "disallow" these activities from consuming your time, energy and enthusiasm. Make the change internally, and the external barriers will dissipate. Follow that? You have a choice in how you want to live, so if something negates your drive, change your perception and move forward. Make the decision that no "thing" will run your life. A light ship is a fast ship.

Sometimes when we begin to "lose the weight," we have a strong reaction because we think external appearances make up who we are. This is not the case. The kind of car you drive doesn't define you. Where you live doesn't define you. The brands of clothes you wear won't define you either. Nothing defines you except your true authentic self. You are the beginning and the end of who you are. You see, the sooner you get rid of things that pull you down, the sooner you'll be able to reach the stream of your dreams. Drop the weight and don't look back.

I think we all can agree that we are here for a reason; essentially, everyone feels they have some sort of calling in life. The trick for most of us is discovering exactly what that calling or purpose is. I can assure you this; nobody can answer that question for you. Don't look to your boss, your friends, or even your parents for the answer, because this answer comes from deep inside of your soul. You have a choice as to what kind of person you want to be. If you can imagine it, you can become it. If you can imagine a new you, a new you will happen. Determine the "who," and the "how" will soon follow. I'll say this again: the main ingredient behind an authentic desire is trust. You have to trust in yourself and the decisions you're making. There is no way around this, either. Trust has to be at your core. Otherwise, you might as well live it up in the stagnant waters of the status quo because without trust, you can't move forward. Are you living with trust in your life, or are you still living the lies of deception and misconception supplied to us through propaganda and media exploitation. Trust first and foremost. How do you expect others to trust in you if you aren't willing to trust yourself?

Usually the desire to be something *more* in life centers on the jobs we pursue. Is your desire to be *more* driven by authenticity or status? Do you desire to do the work or are you snagged by a catchy "title" on your business card? What truly matters in life is how you feel inside, not the rank you keep. How you feel inside determines how you move through life. Truth be told, it really doesn't matter what you do for a living as long as you *love* what you choose. Whether it's a plumber, a baker, or a clown suit maker, the important element to consider is your commitment. What are you willing to commit your time to? What are you willing to commit your soul to? If you're willing to commit but aren't sure what it is you want to do, then think of something that excites you. Think of something that causes you to do your best work. What is your best work? Are you asking these types of questions?

One of the problems most people face when they search for their dream stream is they aren't willing to answer the call when they feel it. They don't answer the door when opportunity knocks. Usually when they feel a pull toward something, self-doubt creeps in and they immediately give up. Never give self-doubt the power to defeat you. Remember, this is a fear-based thought that carries no weight in your new style of thinking. Pinpoint your calling and follow through. When you follow through with your calling, your journey through life is filled with gratification and joy because you're answering the call. You fall in love with your life. Learning how to give and receive love is what life is all about, so listen to your heart and get what you want out of you. This love starts with falling in love with your self. This does not mean you should become self-centered or selfish, this merely means having an authentic appreciation of who you are. That is your base. Once this is achieved, you'll notice how all the other things in life begin to fall into place. Growing up is nothing more than discovering the ability to define your life. You see, I love what I do. I'm in the stream of my dreams. I'm a filmmaker. I'm a screenwriter. And now, I'm an author. I am constantly defining and redefining who I am. That's the exciting thing for me, discovering new territories and embracing the unknown. I'd go crazy, and sometimes I do, if I can't express all the love that is inside of me. If you feel it, answer the call with action and fall in love.

When you fall in love with your choices, you'll begin to notice that work is no longer work. When you are in love with what you have chosen to do, it becomes your dream job. You see? When you are driven by passion rather than a paycheck, your heart widens and you become available for miracles to happen. Don't like your job? Change it. Don't like your position in life? Change it. Summon the courage from within and go for it. Can you imagine a world where everyone loved what they did for a living? Can you imagine a life where passion, love, bliss, creativity, happiness and joy defines the very essence of your life? It's time for you to stop imagining it and start living it. How do you make that happen? Make a decision in your favor and leave behind the fear, doubt and worry of what might go wrong if you do what you want. Focus on the possibilities. Focus on the realization of your dreams. When you're in the stream of your dream, all you can see is the love in your life. You'll begin to notice all the joy, bliss, and creativity that were always there, waiting for you to enjoy. You'll begin to wonder, where has all this love been? It's always there, it's just your attention was simply misdirected. Shift your perception to the good and you'll begin to notice that negativity and self-doubt no longer have a playground in your life. The next time something tries to move you out of your love consciousness, ask yourself these types of questions: "Does it really matter? Will it matter next week? Will it matter a year from now?" Resist the urge to fire the one-fingered salute on the highway of life and drive on. Never die on the sword for anything other than the love you wish to express or accept. Nothing else matters when you're in love.

Have you ever seen the movie *The Rookie*, starring Dennis Quaid? Dennis plays an aging high school baseball coach in a small, dusty town in Texas. Coach is a guy who used to throw a ninety-eight-mile-an-hour fastball back when he was in college. His future looked bright, but an unfortunate injury in college forced him to give up his dream of playing in the big leagues. Instead of finding a well-paying job, he took a coaching job at the high school. Although he loved his life and his family, his old dream never ceased to haunt him. It was a dream that would never come true. That's a tough pill to swallow.

One day, while he was throwing batting practice to the team, his cocky shortstop dared him to fire one in. Coach reared back and blew the pitch right past him. Thinking it was a fluke, the shortstop asked for it again. Pitch after pitch, Coach threw the heat past the entire team. He threw for hours and amazingly, his arm didn't hurt. When the team lost their next game, Coach administered a good old-fashioned tongue-lashing. The topic at hand was becoming great at what you do. He said that they had given up in the game, and that they didn't care. A voice from the back of the room piped up and said, "You're one to talk." The cocky shortstop stood up and said, "You gave up on your dream. How can you stand there and say we're giving up on ours?" A few debating words went back and forth before a deal was struck. If the team won the division title, Coach would attend the next open tryouts for the major leagues.

Long, inspiring story short, the team held up their end of the bargain and won the division title. So, with his four-year-old daughter and infant son in tow, Coach went to the tryouts. The other players viewed him as a joke as he waited around all day for his chance to throw. Finally, when the sun was setting over the Texas plains, Coach got his shot. With radar guns poised, the scouts couldn't believe their eyes as the results came in. A man in his forties was throwing a ninety-eight-mile-an-hour fastball, over and over again. Thinking it was a fluke, the scouts made him continue to throw. He was drafted that summer and pitched in the major leagues for two seasons.

Do you think Coach would have ever realized his child-hood dream if he had spent his time in a "good-paying job"? You see, by taking the job as a high school baseball coach, he was remaining in the stream of his dream. It was a far-off stream from the majors, but he was still in the stream of baseball on a daily basis. He respected himself so much that he wouldn't turn away from a sport that he loved with his heart. He loved the game of baseball, and that's what made him happy. Isn't that what life is all about? Loving something? Being happy? What good does a big house and a luxury car bring if you aren't happy with who you are? The one thing I really love about the movie is that it was based on a true story. It actually happened. An aging high school baseball coach pitched in the major leagues for two years.

You see, our lives are an amazing thing! It's happening right now. Read that line again. Your life is happening *right now!* If we won't celebrate it, who will? Don't wait for praise from other people to see how great you are. You want to be great? Then be great! Start right now. Put yourself in the stream for *your* greatness, and *know* that you're great. It's a power that we're discovering moment by moment. We can choose what we want in our lives. I'm not talking about choosing a Ferrari, either. It's a knowing, not a showing. I'm talking about choosing our innermost desires, our dream of dreams.

Someone might say, "I'm in the stream of my dream, but nothing's happening." This might be a valid point, but you're missing the big picture. It's important to understand that when you're in the stream of your dreams, the stream *is* the dream. Your dream isn't the destination. Your dream is the journey. The day-to-day activity of your dream *is* the dream. If we choose to recognize our dreams only when extreme results occur, we're missing out on the dream itself. The hills and the valleys are what make up the dream. One can't exist without the other. Furthermore, greatness and miracles are something we cannot manipulate or put a clock on. All things happen in their own time. Pushing the natural flow of things will only cause your stream to flow with murky waters. Murky waters will only hinder your ability to see. If you can't see, then how can you be?

For some sad reason, we're seeing a growing number of people who never dive into their dream stream because they can't make a decision. The power of decision is a wonderful thing and should be embraced. Yes, some decisions are difficult, but if you *don't* make a decision, you're allowing someone or some "thing" to make it for you. If you're having trouble answering the question of what career might serve your best interests, I suggest Richard Bolles' wonderful book, *What Color Is Your Parachute?* This book was required reading while I was in college and it helped me solidify my choice to go into the entertainment business. This was my dream stream choice. It was my heart's choice. The money choice for me would have been a career in sales and advertising. Always be careful of dreams that center on money. Money dreams have the ability to leave a person emotionally bankrupt once the goal of money is achieved. As my grandma once told me, "Follow your heart and the money will come."

Making decisions with your heart is exemplified in the story of a friend of mine named Elizabeth. Now, Elizabeth loved essential oils. She absolutely loved wearing oils and diffusing oils. She would even use them to promote physical and psychological well-being. Well, Elizabeth put a lot of love and care into her garden at her home in Venice, California. It was here that she began to grow the plants that would ultimately serve as the foundation for the life she leads now. She began to grow the raw materials for the essential oils she used in order to save money, because these oils can be expensive. Lavender, rosemary, and sage were some of her favorites. Soon enough, she began to realize that her nine-to-five job was only making her money and not serving her heart. She further recognized the profitable mark-up for essential oils. She knew that she loved being in the garden, so she began to think of ways to be more in the stream of her dreams.

Elizabeth did some research and discovered that the best climate to grow lavender was in the Pacific Northwest. She quit her job and moved to Bellingham, Washington, where she now farms an orchard of lavender. She manufactures lavender products and attends the annual lavender festivals that line the Olympic Peninsula. Would you consider this to be a lofty dream? I wouldn't because once she finally discovered the thing that moved her heart—being in the garden—her decision was clear. Now she has more time on her hands than she ever did working in the corporate world, and she's twice as happy. She has a better quality of life because she dove into her stream and didn't question it. She didn't question it because it was an authentic desire from her heart. The money was a by-product of her desire. She found a way to make it happen and dove into the stream.

How do you start a path of heart-filled happiness in your life? Simply put, you can't make a change in your life until you make a decision. Start by thinking about the things that make you happy. What makes your heart move? Once you determine what makes you happy, find your niche. What is your place in the world? What are you good at? What do you want to become good at? Don't put the horse in front of the cart and try to figure out how you'll do something before you know what it is you want to do. Discover the *what* and the *how* will soon follow. Probably the most important element in the dream stream equation is trust. You must trust in your decision. Trust in who you are, and trust in the dreams you dream. Looking for support with your dream? Look within. If you don't believe it, why should anyone else? External support occurs when people see the authenticity in your thoughts, words and actions. If you want to be something more, then do it. Your destiny is not fixed, so stop thinking that it is. If you want something badly enough, it can happen despite what you might think. Negative affirmations of "I can't do this" and "I can't do that," serve nobody, especially your dream stream. Did you know the little voice quoting those negative affirmations is just as capable of telling you "I *can* do this," and "I *can* do that?" All *you* have to do is to shift your level of awareness and focus with positive affirmations. Learn how to think in a way that serves the "I *can*," "I *will*," and "I *am*" principles.

It's up to *you* how *you* view your stream. You can live in fear, or you can live in the excitement of the unknown. Trust in the knowing that the more your heart widens, the more in love with your life you will become. Don't you think it's important to be in love with who you are? Don't you think it's important to celebrate who you are becoming? The answer is always yes. When in doubt, answer YES! Yes will show you the way. Love will show you the way. Your heart will show you the way. Are you ready to listen? Are you ready to dive into the stream of your dreams?

### Chapter 1 Exercise

## Dive Into Your Dream Stream!

The time has come for you to make some decisions. I want you to list five different dream jobs you have for yourself. Take some time out from your busy schedule and visualize these dream jobs. Visualize yourself doing the things you dream of. If you dream of one day owning a bakery, what good does it serve your dream if you're working in the corporate world because it's a "good job?" If you want to own a bakery, work at a bakery. Manage a bakery. This way you're being paid to learn. You're getting a free education on the inner workings of owning and managing a bakery.

By putting yourself in the stream of your dream, you're allowing the universe to work in your favor. You never know what might happen. Maybe the bakery owner might one day have a desire to retire from the baking business and offers either a partnership or the opportunity to buy them out. If you hadn't been in the stream of your dream, you would've missed the opportunity to become a bakery owner, right? See the secrets to the dream stream? You have to be in it for it to work in your favor. Dive in—your life is waiting.

## My Dream Jobs:

1. _____

2. _____

3. _____

4. _____

5. _____

# 2

$\mathcal{T}$he Other P.M.S.

## *Your positive mental state*

Researchers and scientists will always agree on the psychological rewards of exercise. It has been proven that as we exercise, the body produces all sorts of beneficial chemicals. The most commonly known are endorphins. The word endorphin is abbreviated from *"endogenous morphine"* which is a naturally produced morphine by the body through exercise. There are many types of endorphins, but the popular and most effective is the beta-endorphin. The beta-endorphin is responsible for the "euphoric feeling" we have after exercise. In short, endorphins block the signal of pain to the nervous system.

The by-product to this pain blocking is feeling good. Exercise can soon become a way of life because we become "endorphin junkies." Who doesn't like to feel good? Through this "feeling good" from exercise, we develop a stronger sense of self, and adopt a "can do" attitude because it "feels good." This attitude, or Positive Mental State (P.M.S.) as I like to call it, directly affects how we approach our lives. Eating right and getting enough rest is a start, but we need exercise to fuel our dreams. Fitness mogul Jack La Lanne (www.jacklalanne.com) once said during a lecture, "You wouldn't wake your dog up in the morning and give him coffee, a donut, and a cigarette, would you?" It's amazing what we put into our bodies when you think about it. If you put garbage in, you're going to get garbage out. Balanced eating and regular exercise has a direct effect on how you feel. If your body feels better, your mind will follow. Think about it. Who's more productive, the person who lounges on the couch with a bag of potato chips in their spare time, or the person who increases their oxygen intake through exercise?

"I can't work out, I don't have time." "I can't play basketball, I don't know how to dribble." "I can't jog, my knees are bad." "I can't ride a bike, I don't have a bike." It's amazing to see the lengths we'll go to in order to talk ourselves out of something. This style of thinking kills our motivation. Know this: Living in a positive light takes practice. The more we practice, the more it becomes second nature. When we practice, we are no longer thinking about what we should do, because we're already doing it. If you think Barry Bonds just one day decided to break Mark McGwire's major league home-run record, you're sadly mistaken. He practiced, and "it" happened. I think it's time we lose the word "can't" from our vocabulary altogether. It has no business in this new style of thinking so let's kick it to the curb. Through society, our parents, and childhood experiences, we have developed this shadow of doubt on the possibilities of our lives. Why is it that we can think of a million reasons why we *can't* do something, but we have trouble finding one reason why we *should* do something? Have we become that lazy with our lives?

Getting into shape or staying in shape is hard work. I know, because I go through it all the time. I'm an avid mountain biker, but sometimes I just don't feel like going on a ride. I never guilt myself into going, but there's no other form of exercise I love more than biking. Conquering a huge climb is simply empowering. As the miles click by and my anaerobic threshold elevates, something happens. I begin to see my life with more clarity. Just like a car after a tune-up, I'm able to perform and evaluate life on a higher level. I also find that the more I practice my riding, the easier it becomes.

Just a few months ago I went on a ride that not only inspired me but changed my life forever. It was on a trail so deadly that it has claimed the psyches of countless riders across California's Southland. The trail is known as the Bulldog Motorway. Nestled in the hills of Malibu Creek State Park is where you'll find this eight-mile monster, noted in the local riding books as "difficult with a relentless climb." After experiencing Bulldog, I can think of no other word worthy of its description as "relentless." I had heard the buzz around the bike shop about Bulldog, but I never imagined it could be as bad as it actually was.

It was 5:30 in the morning when I met my friend Jim in the parking lot of the park. Now, I must tell you a few things about Jim. He's a good kid, and to know him is to love him; but there's something more. He's got a way of getting up for the moment. This particular morning was no exception. He showed up with his car stereo blaring classical music, a cup of coffee in his hand, and full of life. It was *5:30* in the morning. He was way too jovial, but I loved it.

The morning was dark and dripping with fog. Full of anticipation, we clipped our shoes into our pedals. These clips, which aren't for everyone, ensure an efficient transfer of power from the biker's legs to the bike's power train. Securely fastened, we rode off into the gothic setting that could have been a set for a Tim Burton movie. Conversation was kept to a minimum as we got into the ride. Somewhere around the sixth mile, the beast stood there before us, showing us its ugly teeth. Recent torrential Southland rains had transformed this already deadly ride into a muddy nightmare. We proceeded, with enthusiasm still shining bright. Like most mountain bikers, we had originally agreed that we were going to take it easy today and go for a light spin. Yeah, right. We both knew it was hammer time, because there's no feeling as empowering as riding a bike up a steep hill. Not just riding up a steep hill, but riding *fast* up that hill. That's an incredible feeling.

I waited to see how Jim would approach the hill, and after the first three miles, it was evident that Jim's claim of wanting to take a light spin was legitimate, because I soon passed him. As I pitched myself alone against the beast, the ride turned into something personal. I set a personal goal to not "clip out" of my pedals until I reached the summit. That goal would prove to be the one thing that almost killed me that day. I was about eight miles into the ride and feeling audacious. I was chewing up this so-called "relentless" climb like it was a piece of bubble gum.

Unfortunately, as often happens to people with cocky attitudes, the universe began to slap me around, and I started to feel the pain that Bulldog inflicts. My side began to ache, and the heart monitor climbed to 188 beats per minute (bpm). I couldn't understand it. Was it too much oxygen? Not enough water? Not enough potassium? Or could it be that my goal was too far ahead of my conditioning? Never! I refused to give up. I pulled out an energy bar and bit off a huge chunk. Good move? More carbohydrates to power me through? Wrong! I don't know if you've ever eaten one of these things, but sometimes it can be like eating a wad of tile caulking. So now on top of my side ache, I had a wad of tile caulking about the size of a softball lodged in my throat. I kept thinking there was no way I could continue—it's over, clip out.

My legs had a mind of their own, though, and somehow they powered ahead with the cadence of the wheels. They were spinning as if they felt no pain. Inside of me, however, a battle raged. My body and my ego were battling back and forth. I thought to myself, "Oh God, I'm dying, I have to stop." My heart rate monitor showed 194 bpm. "No! Keep going," my ego said. My side was killing me. "Clipping out just once is okay; this is Bulldog, after all." "Come on, Eric, you don't have to hammer all the time." "No, you can make it." "You can't make it. Give up." Back and forth it went, my thoughts betraying me as mind and body collided.

I then remembered what I had written the day before in my journal: "Never allow 'I can't' to kill your motivation." So I pressed on, despite my elevating pain. Was this ego, or goal realization? I didn't know. Maybe it was a little bit of both. About a mile later, still agonizing in pain, I thought of that nursery story about the train: "I think I can, I think I can." I changed it slightly and came up with "I think I can, I know I can, I will, I will, I am, I am!" Over and over I chanted and before I knew it my side stopped aching, the softball turned into a double play, and I was nearing the top of the hill, with not as much as a single toe touching Bulldog's nasty floor.

With a mile to go, the ride seemed more like a game, and I was feeling ripe. Who said this Bulldog Motorway was a tough ride? Pedals drove around and around, until there it was, right before me. The morning sunrise! I couldn't believe it. I was breaking through the marine fog layer. I was breaking through to a new me. I saw things from a new vantage point, as if I were seeing for the very first time. I stood up and began to sprint even harder. *Drive, drive, drive,* the heart monitor rang up to 196 bpm, but it didn't matter. I made it! I had achieved what I set out to do. It was such a great victory and I was the only person in the race. It was a race against a "can't" style of thinking.

As my feet gripped the ground for the first time in over an hour, I felt one of the most incredible rushes of personal accomplishment in my life. It was such a great victory. Not because I left my buddy behind, not even because I gratified my ego, but because I conquered the style of thinking that kills motivation. I knew I was onto something that day. I knew this ride was going to change my life. It did. About fifteen minutes later, Jim peddled up, rewarded with the same spectacular view of the Southland. Soaking up the heavenly view, we sat in the silence of appreciation. I'll never forget that day. It was the day my life began . . . again.

I have shared this story with you to show how our physical goals and conditioning are directly correlated to our psychological well-being. A healthy body contributes to a healthy mind. When struggle presents itself in our daily lives, we can use the tools we learn from physical conditioning to pull us through. When I was climbing Bulldog, struggle presented itself, but I moved past it with a "can do" attitude even though I wanted to quit. Who knows—maybe next time my mind will want to quit and my legs will pull me through. It's a partnership you *must* enter into. The body and mind are one. If one is out of sync, the other can't function at its optimum performance level.

### Chapter 2 Exercise
### Get Off the Couch!

*WARNING: Before you begin any sort of exercise program, you should consult your doctor and discuss a routine that will best serve you. What works for one person might not work for another.*

Lose the mentality that elicits thought patterns like "I want to get into shape" or "I want to lose weight." Being in shape and being healthy is a way of life, not a destination. It's a journey, much like our lives. If our bodies feel great, our minds will follow. Your exercise for this chapter is to commit to some type of physical activity. Join a gym, ride your bike, walk after dinner, or practice yoga. It doesn't matter; just do something. The more you do, the more you'll desire to accomplish. If you have an aversion to exercise, pass up the elevators of life and take the stairs. If you have a problem climbing two flights of stairs, you know your body needs work. At first you'll begin to notice how quickly you become winded, but don't stop moving your feet. When you feel like you want to give up, push past the feeling and find your second wind, even if it's just two more stairs. Every time you do an exercise, it becomes easier. "Most people never run far enough on their first wind to find out they've got a second. Give your dreams all you've got and you'll be amazed at the energy that comes out of you." – William James (1842–1910), psychologist and author.

# 3

# $\mathcal{D}$on't Miss Your Conscious Bliss
## *The art of waking up*

Don't you just love the way the words *conscious* and *bliss* sound together? I think the undercurrent of this book is the simple notion that we all have a choice in how we want to view our lives. The road through time can be either a joyous and loving experience or a laboring struggle. It's up to you. What is your journey like? What do you see for yourself? Dr. M. Scott Peck (www.mscottpeck.com) might have said it best in his renowned best-selling book, *The Road Less Traveled:* "Life is difficult." Yes, life can be difficult, but let's add something to the end of that sentence: "Life is difficult, but full of opportunities."

The secret to recognizing opportunity is to make sure our journey is a conscious one. That may sound silly to some, but it's true. Too many people in this world are sleepwalking into the routine that life and society has laid out for them. That's okay for some, but I'd rather be awake and aware when I'm talking about moving toward my dreams. My life is important enough to me that I want to assume an active, participatory role in it. I refuse to become a creature of habit and allow routine to stagnate my life. I'm always looking for new ways to learn, and I love that. What about you? Have you stopped learning? Are you taking classes? Are you reading? Do you have some activity that you love to do? Or, are you watching the vacuous stream of propaganda flow through the television set on a daily basis?

It's hard to pinpoint what drives a person to succeed. For some, money is a motivator, and that's fine. We all need money to get by. But if money is at your core, then you can be confident that there's trouble waiting around the corner. Money is an object that can only buy other objects. Money is temporary. It comes and goes. Have you ever noticed how some people attach their happiness to the rise and fall of the stock market? I don't know about you, but I'd rather have something infinite at my core. Something as infinite as love, joy, bliss, gratitude, or acceptance will always trump the dollar bill. If we attach ourselves to an infinite, the abundance factor will follow. Remember, money is a by-product of our dreams.

One of the main reasons we have breakdowns on the road of discovery of conscious bliss is that we aren't solid in our decisions as to where it is we're going. I have some friends that are all over the map with their lives. One day it's this, the next day it's that. Look at how popular the sporting goods business is in our society. Corporations are cashing in on the simple fact that people are fickle. If you add lazy to the equation, look out. One week yoga is all the rage, the next it's the new abdominal rolling machine that promises rock hard abs in only five minutes. What do people do? They rush out and buy a new enthusiasm. You can't buy enthusiasm. Authentic enthusiasm comes from being in love with who you are and discovering your heart's desire. Become solid in your goals and the direction you choose to pursue these goals. Most people give up on something before they have a chance to become great at it. If you want to be great at lawn darts, first you have to ask yourself, "Is this what I really want to do with my life? Do I want to become the world's best lawn dart player?" Of course, this is a silly example, but you get the idea. When we make a choice about something, we have to stick to it. Greatness doesn't happen overnight. I love the saying,

"He's an overnight success that took ten years." I'm working on my fourteenth year.

When you begin the search for your conscious bliss, you must learn to achieve a focus. *Webster's Dictionary* lists the following definitions for "focus": *1. The concentration of attention or energy on something. 2. Maximum clarity or distinctness of an idea.* Focus is vital to living in a state of conscious bliss. Focus is vital to success. Basically, focus is vital to *anything* you want to accomplish in life.

Imagine the focus Tiger Woods has perfected over the years in the game of golf. Thousands of people crowded around to watch him hit a golf ball? What about Laker superstar Kobe Bryant stepping to the foul line with no time on the clock in a game seven of an NBA Championship? You think Tiger and Kobe can execute what they have to do if they didn't achieve a piercing focus? They aren't thinking of anything but accomplishing the task at hand. Life is full of distractions. It's up to you to determine whether or not you want to be distracted. Learn to focus on your dream with maximum clarity. Teach your mind to think in a way that keeps your passion in the forefront of who you are—and more importantly, to keep your eyes fixed on who it is you want to become. The only time focus is pulled away from your dream is when *you* allow it. You have the power to ignore focus pullers.

Ever heard this one? "The average human being uses somewhere in the neighborhood of ten percent of their brain." Ever wonder what it would be like if we could expand our minds an extra one percent? The world is already full of "ten percenters." *Why not* live with a higher level of consciousness? *Why not* separate ourselves from the sleepwalking mumblers, fumblers, and stumblers of life? We can have compassion for them, but it doesn't mean we have to join the misery, does it?

Imagine the possibilities. Imagine what might happen. Imagine what will happen. Imagine what can happen. Push your thoughts to the edge of possibilities and step forward.

It occurs to me that my last paragraph might seem discriminatory against those who choose not to go for that extra percent in life. Please don't think of it like that. Of course, some people are satisfied with ten percent. Some people are okay with "working for a living." I prefer to think of my life as living my dreams as opposed to "working for a living." The more I discover about my own consciousness, the more I want. The more love I feel, the more I want to express. It's all about staying focused. Stay conscious of your passions. Stay on track and live your dreams. Don't settle for "working for a living." Desire a job that is a deeper love. A job that pulls you out of bed in the morning is much more exciting than "work," don't you think?

Achieving a higher level of consciousness is available to everyone if they are willing to look past the surface of their daily lives. This surface is the garbage that we have been brainwashed to believe and desire. Thoughts of accumulation have nothing to do with personal success or achieving a higher level of consciousness. Remember, no "thing" defines who you are. One secret to this consciousness we're talking about is to feed your mind with positive thoughts, words, and actions. Some people think you're either born with inspiration and enthusiasm or you aren't. That's an assumption and we all know where that gets us. Even the inspired have a desire to become inspired. For example, I remember one Sunday morning a few months ago when Tony Robbins was visiting Agape. Here is *the* main man in the motivational world, and he's there getting inspired by my minister. We all need a little inspiration now and then. To stay on track, you need to do whatever feeds your motivation.

Read whatever you can get your hands on. Any book from the *Chicken Soup for the Soul* series by Mark Victor Hansen and Jack Canfield would be a great place to start. I remember the day I first met Mark Victor Hansen (www.markvictorhansen.com). I heard we were going to have a guest speaker one weekend and he was the guy who was the driving force behind all the *Chicken Soup* books. I was looking forward to this day. As Mark was introduced, I realized he was the same guy who wore crazy ties to church every Sunday morning. I had been saying good morning to this guy for months and didn't know *he* was the Chicken Soup guy. I loved meeting him officially because here was a guy who looked in the mirror each morning and said, "I love this tie." I love that style of thinking and the freedom it exudes. Mark spoke about discovering the enthusiasm in your life. I felt like he was speaking directly at me because the topic was so timely for this book. Mark has been such an inspiration for me and I love his theme line: "Yes or yes?" Mark is a man who is on fire for who he is. He is a man who lives in the world of all possibilities. You can't help but feel it because he wears it so well. When he and Jack wrote the *Chicken Soup* series, they were turned down by everyone. Thirty nine publishers said no. Nobody thought the idea for *Chicken Soup* was worth the paper it would be printed on. Even their agent left them behind, saying the idea was too lofty. Guess what? That move cost the agent a commission from sales of over five million dollars. To the agent's dismay, the registers are still ringing. *Chicken Soup* is everywhere. Mark's enthusiasm for his life reminds me of my own. He was one of the many inspirations for me to finish this book. His enthusiasm reminds me of how I feel about my life and who I want to become.

Another great starting point is the book I mentioned earlier, *The Road Less Traveled,* by Dr. M. Scott Peck. This book set records for nonfiction, being the number-one best-selling book for twelve years. That is truly amazing. My parents gave me a copy when I was in junior high school and I quickly read it cover to cover. It is a great book that explains a lot about life and the struggles we go through to get what we want. I suggest reading as many of these types of books as you can get your hands on. Attend as many seminars as you can. Go to church. Find a mentor. Get involved with other like-minded individuals. Do whatever you need to do, but get involved with your life. When you become involved with your life, the gateway to your conscious bliss is easier to attain. The key is to find and pursue things that evoke a passionate emotion inside of you. I believe this is vital to attaining our goals. We are here for such a flicker of time, so *why not* go after the finest things we can imagine? Go for the gold ring, but realize that the gold ring has nothing to do with luxury cars or other material trimmings. The gold ring we're speaking of is the conscious bliss and becoming comfortable with who we are. There is nothing more blissful than sitting in the stillness and knowingness of "I love who I am." When that is at your core, nothing can stop you.

Conscious bliss has often been a target of skeptics. The arguments center around statements like, "How do you expect me to go after this conscious bliss and pursue my passions when the bills are due?" This is a valid and realistic point, but you'll be surprised what you can do when you want something badly enough. Ask yourself how badly you want it. If you want to become a veterinarian, then go back to school and become one. Sure, you'll be financially challenged for a while, but that's part of the equation, right? Nothing is free. There's no hitchhiking on the road to your dreams. Do the work and embrace your decision to break free. There are some people who have no problem with putting a $1,500 television on a credit card, but have trouble justifying the cost for a $39-per-unit night class at the community college. What are you willing to do for your dreams? "The difference between 'involvement' and 'commitment' is like an eggs-and-ham breakfast; the chicken was 'involved'—the pig was 'committed.' " – Unknown. Everything worthwhile requires a sacrifice of some kind. You must be committed to your dream.

While I'm going through the journey of becoming who I am, I love the fact that I'm conscious of the journey and not the destination. My attention is on right now and not on some preconceived future bliss. I wouldn't change anything about *right now* because it's just that, right now. If I worried about the money, I'd die from frustration and join the ranks of people who have given up on the movie business. I'll always do what feeds my passions because I love the life that I'm in. I love the man I am. I love being in love with who I am. I know my dream of being a filmmaker is perfect. Why? Because I can see it happening as I'm living it right now. Sure, I'd really love to be directing movies budgeted at fifty million dollars, but I'm in the stream for things to happen, so it's only a matter of time. This is something I know. I'm already doing what I love and let me tell you, there is nothing better than answering your passionate call. Remember, the way you think directly affects the way you act. The way you act directly affects the way the universe reacts. What you say affects what happens. You see? Walk the talk and talk the walk.

The one thing that can keep you from living in a state of conscious bliss is baggage. Some people love their baggage. It can weigh you down so much that you will have trouble standing up straight. If you can't stand up, how can you reach your goals? The funny thing about the past and the emotional baggage associated with it is that we actually believe it has something to do with who we are right now. Trust me, it doesn't. Whatever happened yesterday has no bearing on what can or will happen today. When we dwell on the past, we're ignoring or at the very least, handicapping our future not to mention, interfering with our *right now*. People will lead their lives with statements like: "Can I tell you what happened to me? Can I tell you how difficult my life has been? Can I tell you how I've been mistreated all my life?" This style of awfulizing puts your attention on the wrong vibration. The limitation brought on by living in this victim role only steals your drive to become more of who you really want to be. We can take comfort in knowing that we have a built-in safety net for processing this fear, doubt or worry of the past: No matter what happens, the past can no longer hurt us. The past is the past and that's the beauty of it. You don't have to go through it again if you don't want to. What *has* happened is over. The past has no bearing on *right now*. The past has no bearing on *tomorrow*. If you're dealing with something that is too sensitive to talk about, then write about it, but it is important to get it out so that you can move on. "If you can't get rid of the skeletons in your closet, you'd best teach them to dance." – George Bernard Shaw (1856–1950).

After you get the baggage out of the way, you can begin a journey to your own conscious bliss. To do that, you *must* learn to be comfortable with yourself. That means spending time alone. Now most people hate to be alone, but it's an important practice in which to engage. If you can't "hang" with yourself, how do you expect to hang with other people? Many of us hide in an unconscious state because we're afraid of confronting our own lives. Here's a secret: The sooner you confront your life, the sooner you'll free yourself from the jail in which your perceptions have imprisoned you. This is a very important point to catch and is the very foundation on which a joy-filled life is built. If you have trouble spending time alone with your thoughts, you need to determine why you're feeling this way. More often than not, this uneasy feeling is born out of fear, doubt or worry of some kind. It would be easy for me to simply tell you to discount these feelings and move on, but I'm not going to do that. I'm sure you *think* these feelings are real and, at times, frightening. I'm sure you *think* you don't deserve an all good, all knowing life filled with joy, love, wisdom, creativity, and bliss. As Dr. Michael Beckwith said, "Don't believe everything you think." Imagine if you will the power of your feelings which are based on unconditional love for who you are. There is no fear doubt or worry when love is at the foundation of who you are. In short, it's time to lose the fear of being alone by turning to a solid foundation built on love. It's time to love and appreciate yourself for who you are and who you are becoming.

The burning question remains; are you willing to really listen to your heart? Are you willing to rest in the confidence that the tough questions about your life might have tough answers? Remember, you have nothing to lose when you answer the tough questions, because the answers will lead you to your dreams. The true blessing here is that you are becoming more *aware* of your feelings. Living a life without feeling is like having a car without a steering wheel. You see, to feel is to love. To love is to really live. No matter what you're feeling, good vibrations or bad, be thankful you are actually feeling. You'd be surprised how many people go through life suppressing their feelings. When you feel, you're bringing something into your consciousness and by doing that, you're one step closer to the life you dream of. That's the crux of becoming conscious: listening to your feelings and then processing your way through them. This is how you become free. This is what conscious bliss is all about, becoming awake and aware of who and what you really are.

Isn't it time to wake up and see your life as if you were seeing it for the very first time? We often take our lives for granted because we're so consumed with the struggles of accumulation. Our attention is on what we don't have or what we didn't get from our parents. It's time to take a step back and really look at your life. Look at all the friends and family you have to be grateful for. Don't wait for a lightning bolt to show how much you love someone. Do it right now. Walk into the next room and tell your family how much you appreciate them. You'll be surprised at how great this makes them feel. It makes you feel pretty good too. Try it.

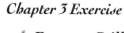

### *Chapter 3 Exercise*

### Become Still and Listen to Your Dreams

Find a quiet place and let your mind go. As you become comfortable, trust in what you're doing by allowing the circumstances and appearances of your life to slip away. Move into a heart space filled with love and compassion and begin to visualize yourself doing the very things you dream about. If you find negativity slipping into your consciousness, gravitate through it with love. Look forward and love. Become conscious of the question, "What have I done today to make my dream become a reality?" Recognize the pitfalls of concentrating on your past and move into the feeling of *right now*. Stop thinking of what *was* and put your attention on what *is*. Write down seven affirmations as to who and what it is you want to become with language that centers on "I am," "I can," and "I will." Listen to the way you talk. Some examples include: "I am a good and loving person." "I am powerful enough to get the job." "I am creative." "I am joy-filled and love follows me everywhere."

## My 7 Affirmations:

1. _____

2. _____

3. _____

4. _____

5. _____

6. _____

7. _____

# 4
# $\mathcal{T}$he Moment of "Ah ha"

## *The day I woke up and said, "Why not?"*

I had just transferred out of the music department, into and out of the theater arts department, before landing in the business marketing department. I was all over the place in college, but I knew I was onto something with this latest move into the business department. I knew I was doing the right thing because my heart told me so. My professors, however, didn't agree, when they discovered that I wanted to make movies after I graduated. "Shouldn't you be in the communications department?" "Shouldn't you be in film school?" Who needs self-doubt when you have professors "advising" you to get out of their class? At first I thought they might've been right, but I knew my inner voice was on the right track. It empowered me through this state of uncertainty—and let me tell you, there is nothing more exciting than conquering self-doubt and embracing your innermost desires. All that is required to accomplish this is trust. You have to trust in yourself. If you don't trust yourself, how do you expect others to trust you? We touched on this in the last chapter's exercise, but trust is everywhere in this new style of thinking you desire.

I knew early on that the road to becoming a filmmaker was going to be a hard one. If we look at the financial "challenges" I currently have, one can say the road is still hard. But let's remember, happiness doesn't have a dollar sign attached to it. I am living my dream every day of my life. Am I rich? Yes,

I'm rich with love. I'm rich with personal happiness. I'm rich with knowing that I'm doing what it takes to become something amazing. I'm rich with possibilities because I'm doing what it takes to become more of who I am. I'm doing what it takes to become extraordinary. So, the answer would be yes, I am rich. The money will come because I'm doing my homework.

Do you remember the girl in school who got the "A" on almost every test? I used to think, "Oh, she's just smart. She knows this stuff already." I soon realized how wrong that statement was. I realized that the girl wasn't given all the answers, and she didn't come by the knowledge through osmosis, either. She just did what we didn't do, which is the homework. Are you doing your homework? Are you taking an active role in becoming who it is you want to become?

When we take a look inside of ourselves and ask the tough questions, we have to possess the courage to answer them. Usually, this is the work that most people will shy away from because we buy into the fear of what we might find. Fear of what we might find? I'll never understand why some people live in fear of becoming successful. Why would any- one engage in self-destructive behavior? Do you know anyone that complains about wanting a better life but continues on a self- destructing path? Nobody is served when you play small in this life. Fear is nothing more than a misguided thought that has gotten away from you. Let's put fear where it belongs, at the curb with the ego. It's time to move forward and capture your dreams. I know this is easier said than done, but fear is a waste of time. Positive attitude is everything and is the perfect place to begin. You see, when we're in a positive mental state, a chain reaction occurs. Thoughts and actions soon follow the attitude and before you know it, you have forgotten what you were afraid of to begin with. "I have often been afraid, but I would not give in to it. I made myself act as though I was not afraid and gradually my fear disappeared." —Theodore Roosevelt (1858–1919).

If you want to become successful in what you desire, you must change your style of living in the world to revolve around success. Your thoughts, words and actions need to be focused on your success. Your vibratory frequency should focus on success. You need to claim it on a daily basis. The best advice I ever got was to surround myself with people who were smarter than I was. Seek out like-minded individuals and form an alliance. Surround yourself with people on the same path that you desire. What good does it do you to hang out with a bunch of Wall Street executives when you would rather build custom homes for a living? Reinforce your dreams with positive affirmations. Define your vibration to serve your dreams, not your fears surrounding lack and limitation.

Remember when our parents would make us try all sorts of things we didn't want or didn't like? Remember when your parents said, "Try it, you'll like it"? My most vivid memories often revolve around nasty vegetables and piano lessons. But maybe, just maybe somewhere in this stream of new experiences, we discovered something that we loved that might've initially frustrated us. I often wonder why we stop this experimental mode simply because we grow older. When we get comfortable with the current state of affairs, we forget to expand our lives and experience new things. Is it because we aren't required to anymore? Did homework put us off so much that we loathe even the thought of working to experience the unknown? Don't be afraid of what you don't know! Read and apply, and you're rewarded with supply. Don't balk when faced with change, because change is growth. Don't you want to grow up? Try it, taste it, embrace it. You never know, you just might grow from it. Better yet, you just might love it.

Don't be afraid of failure either. Failure has gotten a bad rap over the years and it's time to give the poor word its due. Failure is an opportunity, not a stop sign. Get used to it now, because you will fail. I will fail. Some of us will fail again and again, but that's okay because failure is all a part of the growth process. There is always a life lesson to be learned from our failures. The lesson begins with how you deal with failure, how you pick yourself up, how you start again, and the resolve you gain.

A friend of mine, Cynthia Kersey, recently wrote a book called *Unstoppable* which you can find at www.unstoppable.net. This book is a must-read for anyone who wants to see how other people have pushed through adversity. In the book there's a story that I just love. It's the story of a man who decided to become a lawyer at the age of 35. At the time, he had two sons who were in grade school. When his sons were in high school, he finished law school and took the state bar exam. He failed. He took the bar again and again, failing each time. When his sons graduated college, he took the bar exam again. He failed, again. His sons graduated law school. He failed again. He failed while he began working as a clerk for his sons' law firm. Then, one day, at the age of 64, he finally passed the bar exam. When most people were looking to retire, he was starting his career. He had his life's dream to look forward to. He didn't give up, despite a major challenge. Read Cynthia's book. You'll find many more *unstoppable* stories like this one.

Perseverance is where our character is built. The stronger we are in our new style of thinking, the easier the hurdle of failure will be. Whenever I used to complain about something, my father would tell me, "It's good for you. It builds character." I grew to hate those words, but looking back, I now realize how right my father was. In short, he was summarizing the classic learning curve, which states that failure and frustration are catalysts for learning and growth. Failure is trying to teach us something. Be open. Find the message in your failure and press on. Never give up. Remember, persistence overcomes resistance. You have a choice when faced with adversities such as failure. You can either let it overcome you, or you can use it to overcome the challenge at hand. Sounds simple, doesn't it? Well, it isn't. It's hard work. It's the work that most will shy away from. If you aren't willing to sweat for your own successes, who will? *Why not* be the one who makes a difference in your life?

In our old style of thinking, we would kill our ideas and passions before we even gave them a chance to start. For instance, you woke up with this amazing idea and before the day was over, the idea was pushed aside because thoughts like "I can't" and "I don't have" filled your head and destroyed your desires. You have the *power* to shape your own destiny. In addition, you have the *power* to choose the style of your thoughts. You also have the *power* to say what happens in your life. Recognize a pattern here? *You* have the *power* so don't give away this power by giving up.

By not giving up, we remain open and available to the possibilities of what might happen. I've opened myself up for criticism and comparison by writing this book. Readers and critics alike can take their shots. Does that scare me? I think you know the answer to that by now, but I remember when I was doing my research for this book. I went to the Self-Help & Motivation section of the bookstore to see what was being written on the subject. I had to laugh—not at the amount of books I saw on the shelf, because there were many, but at the feeling of intimidation that came over me. I laughed at the fact most of the titles had been written by doctors, psychologists, ministers, celebrities, and anyone else with a set of initials before or after their names. These initials seem to qualify or legitimatize a person to write a book. I laughed because I told myself, *Why not?* I'm qualified to do anything I put my heart into.

I remember having thoughts like, "The book could be a complete failure. I could be rejected by every publisher. I could fall flat on my face." I soon realized that these thoughts were the residual "leftovers" from my old style of thinking. I quickly focused my attention on the land of possibilities. I put my focus on what could be. *Why Not* could be lauded by critics. *Why Not* could help someone at just the right time in their life. *Why Not* might cause *you* to do something amazing with *your* life or might cause someone to achieve a level of personal greatness that they never before thought possible. God only knows what might happen. Can you differentiate between your old style and this new style of thinking? Which would you rather live with? Remember, our thoughts are where we live. Your thoughts are like a house. You wouldn't enter your house with muddy shoes, would you? No? Then don't allow muddy thoughts into your flow of success. Be protective of where you live.

You can do it. I can do it. We can do it together. There can be no failure when you follow your heart. I'm forever changed as a result of following a dream. Based on that, I already have experienced success, right? Whatever happens now is only a by-product of what I'm doing. The only crimes in your life are the passions unlived. Are you living your passions? Are you living your dreams? Are you doing your homework? Time to get busy—your life is waiting!

### Chapter 4 Exercise
## Forward Motion Breeds Devotion!

"Success usually comes to those who are too busy to be looking for it." – Henry David Thoreau (1817–1862). Keep yourself moving forward. If you feel stuck, do something. Find a hobby. Join a local charity. Become a volunteer. Paint the house. Spend time with your family. Just get off the mental couch and get busy! Get up from where you are mentally living and dive in. Feed your mind and find your childlike sense of inspiration. Share and explore. Inspiration is born out of involvement. Passion is born out of practice. If you can't find your inspiration, use the inspiration of others to pull you forward. Surround yourself with people who are in love with what they do. This will cause a desire for action inside of you. You'll soon want to have what they feel for your own life. You'll begin to be pulled by your vision. Don't wait for things to happen — get into the game and mix it up. You never know what you're capable of until you try. Start trying today. What do you want from your life? Write down three things you're willing to commit to within the next 30 days.

**3 Things I'm Willing to Commit to Within 30 Days:**

1. _____

2. _____

3. _____

# 5

## $\mathcal{T}$he Status Quo Woes
### *Breaking free with passion*

At some point in the 1980s, the Nike shoe company coined what might be the ultimate positive-thinking phrase of our time. The "Just Do It" blitz took America by storm. It was everywhere, and is still often quoted in pop culture. The slogan seemed to separate Nike from the rest of the athletic shoe industry, which is probably one of the most highly competitive markets out there, after the soft drink market. With this slogan, Nike managed to capture a feeling that we should adopt in order to succeed. Fittingly, Reebok countered with "Life Is Short, Play Hard." This is another slogan that captures a feeling, and I love them both.

Now, I'm not one to advocate listening to corporate slogans, but I have to admit, these slogans capture the essence of positive thinking. The beauty of these slogans is they reinforce the notion that we can't wait for things to happen *to* us or settling for the status quo's in life. It is our job to make things happen *for* us. If we won't, who will? "Try not. Do. Or do not. There is no try." – Yoda *(Star Wars: Episode V— The Empire Strikes Back © 1980 and 1997).* Now you don't have to be a Jedi Master to realize that this is *your* life to celebrate. This is your life to live to its fullest capacity. *Why not* go for it? *Why not* shoot for the moon? One of the main reasons we have problems making changes in our lives — changes that move us in the direction of our dreams — is complacency with the status quo. We become comfortable in the routine of life, and the thought of change is either frightening or just too much work to deal with. Statements like "This is good enough" wedge their way into our consciousness and before we know it, our lives become "good enough." We abandon the desire to be more, and slip into a cerebral nothingness and a life of summer re-runs. When the hunger for personal greatness is never satisfied, the hunger pangs pass and years begin to click away. No, no, no! It's important to seize the day and stave off any regret that you gave up on your dreams! Become conscious of any future regret from giving up before you give up! See yourself living your dreams.

We need to be conscious of what we say — and more importantly, how we say it. We must heed our own thoughts, words, and actions. Have you ever noticed the reaction you get when someone disrespects you? Usually, you won't stand for it. The first thing you say is, "Hey, you can't talk to me that way. Who do you think you are?" This scenario happens all the time: Someone spews some sort of garbage your way, and you just won't put up with it. I applaud this behavior of not putting up with it. However, I don't understand why we'll put up with that sort of talk from ourselves when we're pursuing our dreams. We'll say things to ourselves that we would never tolerate from other people. Why is that okay? Are we not good enough to receive the same respect from ourselves that we expect from other people? The answer is no! If you want respect from other people, *why not* start with yourself?

Why are people comfortable with old problems? *Why not* embrace new horizons and new solutions, leaving behind the comfort zones of a painful life? In order to move out of the status quo, we need to incorporate positive, affirming behavior. It doesn't happen overnight. I like to make a little game out of it with myself. As I become more and more cognitive of the power my thoughts, words and actions carry, I'll catch myself when I slip. I catch myself with a smile of recognition and gratitude. I catch myself knowing that old habits die hard. They die hard, but I make sure that they indeed do die. We all slip from time to time, but the important thing is what you do after the slip. I remember laughing to myself the other day as I became agitated with a customer service representative over my cellular service. I knew it was happening. I knew I was losing my patience as I waited on hold for what seemed like forever. I became aware of my old habits of reactive anger and remembered what I had written only hours before. I laughed because the old me would've sent the poor customer service rep into the depths of oblivion for the way I was being treated. My laughter brought forward my smile and I knew exactly how to deal with the customer service rep when she came back to the phone. I was as sweet as could be, and you know what? I got what I wanted because of the way I treated her. We get out of life what we put into it. I moved out of my status quo and into love and compassion and that's exactly what I got. I soon realized what is meant by "You'll catch more flies with honey than you will with vinegar." I recognized that my position of happiness was being compromised by my cell phone service, or lack of it in this case.

Californians will know that in Los Angeles, the mere thought of the San Diego Freeway will cause anyone to lose it. The 405/101 freeway interchange is the busiest section of highway in the entire United States. I drive it once a week, and when I do, I see words like "You *#&$!" and "%#$@!" fly from the lips of drivers who are caught in the rat race maze of the go, go, go. The only outcome of road rage or any other anger-based, ego-based, negative-based "thing" is that we lose our blissful state of consciousness. That doesn't serve anything.

It certainly doesn't serve us effectively, does it? The next time you feel a shift from your conscious blissful state of who you are and who you are becoming, move into a space of love and compassion. As you continue this practice, love and compassion will be the qualities that dominate your life. Don't ever rest in the status quo. Don't ever let someone else or some "thing" dictate how you feel. You're the pilot of this plane; how are you choosing to fly?

Remember the saying, "Things happen for a reason"? What would you say if you discovered a traffic jam was actually the universe working to your advantage? When that person cut you off two intersections ago, putting you behind a whole ten seconds, you were being saved from a huge cement truck that will run the red light five miles ahead of where you are now. So, by making you ten seconds late, you "see" the cement truck running the red light instead of actually being hit by it. Is this too much of a lofty example for us to consider? *Why not* make sense of the chaos with something as beautiful as the notion that the person was actually a guardian angel? Still too lofty? *Why not* find enjoyment in the things you can't change? Honking, shaking your fist, cursing, and throwing the one-fingered salute serves nothing, especially your state of love. With all the road-rage accidents and altercations I see on TV, I'll continue to think of these lofty examples and resist the one fingered salute. *Why not* think differently? *Why not* rest in your blissful state of consciousness and *love* the fact that someone put you ten seconds behind? You never know what ten seconds might mean to your life. After all, it is just ten seconds. To help us realize the value of time, let's look at the following list:

✦ To realize the value of one year: Ask a student who just failed a final exam.

✦ To realize the value of one month: Ask a mother who has given birth to a premature baby.

✦ To realize the value of one week: Ask an editor of a weekly newspaper.

✦ To realize the value of one day: Ask a daily-wage laborer who has 7 kids to feed.

✦ To realize the value of one hour: Ask the lovers who are waiting to meet.

✦ To realize the value of one minute: Ask a person who has missed the train, the bus, or the plane.

✦ To realize the value of one second: Ask a person who has survived an accident.

✦ To realize the value of one millisecond: Ask the person who has won a silver medal in the Olympics.

*"Time waits for no one. Yesterday is history. Tomorrow is a mystery. Today is a gift. That is why it is called the present. Treasure every moment you have. You will treasure it even more when you can share it with someone special." – Unknown.*

Become thankful for what you have in your life. More importantly, we should be thankful and willing to accept the things we know nothing about. The reason people love to rest in the status quo is because stepping out of it requires change. Change causes a gambit of emotions in everyone, because we're leaving behind something familiar. Be careful of familiarity because it can lull you to sleep. Before you know it, you'll be sleepwalking through life and wonder, "where did the time go?" Break out and discover new gifts and talents in your life. Keep your eyes and ears open, and *act* on your instincts to grow. Go after your desires and *just do it*. Push yourself to the next level in the pursuit of your personal greatness.

Try surrounding yourself with people who are passionate about what they do and who they are. Ever notice what it's like to be around someone alive and full of energy? You can't help but find energy and vitality for your own life. Listen to how they talk. Watch them interact with other people. You can't help but be inspired. On the other hand, how do you feel when you're around someone who is negative and filled with pessimism? Things like "I can't," "I don't have," "I won't," and "that's stupid" dominate their language. Sooner or later, they'll scrutinize *your* goals and the dreams you have. If you listen long enough, you might start to believe what they say about you. What then? It's back to a life where your biggest concern is what's on cable TV every night. "Keep away from people who try to belittle your ambitions. Small people always do that, but the really great ones make you feel that you, too, can become great." – Mark Twain (1835–1910). In the blink of an eye, time travels by. You don't have time to be negative or listen to negative people. *Go* and *get* what you want out of life and fire up to be whatever it is *you* want to be! Remember, *you* get out of life what *you* put into it! Invest in yourself! Invest in your future! Invest in the desire to be more by stepping out your status quo surroundings!

Prepare yourself for the greatness that is going to happen in your life. Don't be left on the doorstep when opportunity knocks. How do you prepare yourself? You follow your heart. You follow your innermost desires and never allow inhibition about doing something that you've never done before kill your drive. Ever have an impulse to dance with your lover in the middle of a crowded room, even if there's no music? What about the impulse to skip down the street with a friend? For those men out there who are worried about skipping down the street for no reason, haven't you heard? Real men skip. Ever get a silly impulse? Did you do anything about it, or did you worry what people might think if you did? These examples are merely the tip of the iceberg of what we're talking about in this chapter. If you can't answer the small, silly, impulsive calls of stepping out of the box, how do you expect to make the life-changing steps you so desperately desire? Start somewhere.

Unfortunately, for most people, the silly impulse is killed by the "responsible adult" inside them. Actually, the responsible adult would answer the call, because the responsible adult would never ignore a childlike desire or impulse because of what someone might think. The responsible adult has no fear of what other people might think. For some reason, society has put a dimmer switch on the inner child. We've been over this before, but who cares what someone else thinks of you? All we have to do is go back to trust. Trust in your desires. Trust and answer the call from the child within, because children lead with their hearts. Want to learn how to be a "responsible adult?" Want to learn how to be a real grown-up? Learn from children. Visit a playground and watch how children move through life without judgment. Watch the way love, adventure, and curiosity fills their every move. Watch how friendly and open they are with each other. I never could understand why we can't talk to someone we don't know just because we don't know them. Los Angeles is filled with people who stare at the cement while they walk down the street in order to avoid eye contact with someone they don't know. It's a shame to witness, but I refuse to buy into it. I love people I don't know. How else do you get to know someone unless you talk to them? Resist the resistance and be open. You never know who you might meet.

I recently had the privilege of meeting Terry Cole-Whittaker. Terry is an amazing woman who wrote a book called *What You Think of Me Is None of My Business.* Don't you just love that title? The book is a must-read for anyone who is particularly stuck with worrying other people's opinions. Art Linkletter, Zig Ziglar, Jim Rohn, and Terry Cole-Whitaker were the true pioneers in the motivation movement back in the seventies. I love what Terry's all about, and the title of her book is perfect for us. What other people think of you doesn't matter when you have a "knowing" inside. When you know that you're special, talented, creative, joyful, motivated, child-like and in love, nothing else matters. As you dance in the middle of the room or engage in other childlike impulses, most of the people in the room will wish they had your zest for life. Wives will hit their husbands and say, "How come you're not more like that?" Don't look at it as if they're going to think of you as someone stupid or childish. If that's the way they feel, it's *their* problem—don't let it become yours. Thinking in this negative style will kill your sense of adventure, and most of all, it will kill your sense of drive. Listen to your inner child. Leave behind the comfort of the status quo and dance through the night.

Now, I can't pass up the opportunity to talk about the mysterious panel of judges out there who are behind the statement "You know what *they* say." Would you like to know who "they" are? The answer to the question is who cares? Live your life the way you think it should be lived, with care, consideration, gratitude, and trust. Don't worry about how other people might judge you. The art of worry is a state of uncertainty, and it's a waste of your time. Buying into a "they" mentality is merely a way for those on the fence to be pushed back into their caves and keep the status quo alive. Taking control of your own life is difficult, but the rewards are endless. Just do what you feel inside, and if it feels good, do it even more. Remember, *just do it, life is short, play hard! Why not?*

The inhibitions we have, or that society has placed on us or in us, can be attributed to our desire for peer approval. Peer approval, or "fitting in," is something we've been conditioned to crave as early as elementary school. Everybody wanted to be popular. Everybody wanted to hang out with the prettiest girl or the captain of the football team. This counterfeit but prevalent desire continues through high school and often into college. You were either "in" and knew where all the parties were, or you were "out" and you spent your time trying to get "in." The real "in" starts with who you are. When you have that, which is love, joy, bliss, and your God appearing through you, you *are* the party. Are you ready to celebrate?

I found myself in a limbo-crossover stage throughout my school years. I started to notice it sometime during the transition between junior high school and high school. Suddenly, everyone stopped playing in the band because nobody wanted to be a "band geek." I loved music, and I didn't care if people called me a band geek. I did, however, find it hard to be a crossover kid. I stayed in the jazz and symphonic bands throughout high school, but I also played sports and performed in the theater. I found myself with all different types of friends: the geeks, the jocks, the social "in crowd," and even the nerdy crowd. This continued into college when I joined the Sigma Alpha Epsilon fraternity. I kept my interest in music high on my priority list. After all, I was majoring in music. The brothers of the fraternity hazed me for being in the band because of all the time it required me to be away from the house. I didn't care. This was something that *I* wanted to do. If they wanted to kick me out, so be it, but I wasn't going to quit something I loved because "they" wanted me around for cleanups and other degrading pledge activities.

The following year I added another activity to the mix and auditioned for the winter play. I thought, hey, *why not*, I did some acting in high school, so I'll give it a try. What was the worst thing that could happen? I wouldn't be cast in a part? Well, I did get a part, but this didn't bode well with the "always wear black" members of the theater department, because I was in a fraternity. I was observing discrimination from both sides. They key word there is *observing*. I didn't own it. I was aware of it, but it didn't become a block for my desires. I didn't care what "they" thought. I was following my heart. I applied the same philosophy of "take me as I am" as I did with the fraternity, and I pressed on. It was at this moment I became aware of what I wanted to do in life. I knew putting on some type of production would be my future. I wasn't sure if it was music, theater, or some other art form, but I knew I was on the right track. Imagine if I had folded to the pressure applied by other people. Imagine if I didn't step out of my comfort zone. I might have never discovered my passion for filmmaking. I knew I loved the hard work of rehearsing for a performance. I loved performing. I loved expressing for friends and family. This love soon led me to the realization that television and film were in my future. Here I am. I'm doing what I love to do. I'm expressing my heart. I'm sharing my heart. Do you realize the power in saying things like this? Would you like to?

Do we really care what people think of us? To a certain extent, I think the answer is yes; but if it stops you from your heart's desire, move past the feeling and *just do it*. If you worry about what other people might think of you, you'll never try or experience anything new. Nothing ventured, nothing gained. Listen to your heart. Follow your feelings. Follow your innermost desires and discover your passions. Let go of the status quo and move into your passion. "Greatness is not in where we stand, but in what direction we are moving. We must sail sometimes with the wind and sometimes against it— but sail we must, and not drift, nor lie at anchor." – Oliver Wendell Holmes (1841–1935).

### *Chapter 5 Exercise*
### Check the Score!

There is nothing wrong with the current state of affairs, unless it's keeping you from your dream. Determine what is keeping you from your dream. In order to do this, make a list of negative influences in your life. These are things that keep you from living your dream. Take your time and really be honest with yourself, even if it hurts. Some negative influences might include your job, where you live, a dysfunctional relationship, alcohol or drugs. Now make a second list of influences that drive and empower you towards accomplishing your goals. Empowering influences might include talents you have, your education, where you live, or the support base of family and friends. Now compare the two. If your negative list is bigger than your positive list, you need to make some drastic changes. One by one, begin to eliminate the negative and enhance the positive. Examine each item listed on the negative side and determine what needs to be done to remove it all together. Worried you don't have enough items written down on your positive side? Go back to the drawing board, because you're not looking hard enough. The most positive thing about anyone's life is the fact that they are unique. Embrace the very notion that nobody is like you. Embrace the fact that you're a divine and unique individual who is now ready and willing to do whatever is necessary to make your dreams become your reality.

## Part 1:   NEGATIVE INFLUENCES

1. _____

2. _____

3. _____

4. _____

5. _____

6. _____

7. _____


## Part 2:   POSITIVE INFLUENCES

1. _____

2. _____

3. _____

4. _____

5. _____

6. _____

7. _____

# 6

# *S*tress

## *Is it running your life?*

Somewhere between the years 1275 and 1325, the word *stress* connoted emphasis, strain, fear, or pain. Then, between 1850 and 1855, the term *stressful* was introduced with the meaning "tension." Much later, in the pursuit of finding the quintessential athlete, scientists and health enthusiasts came up with *stress testing*. Stress testing was first conducted between 1970 and 1975, and was designed to put the body through enormous physical exertion while the results were monitored. Somewhere in the early 1980s, pop culture coined the phrase *stressed out.*

We have three forms of stress in our society: acute stress, episodic acute stress, and chronic stress. Most common to our culture is acute stress. This is the everyday stress that causes us to worry about our jobs, a fender bender on the freeway, or "drama" with a friend. Episodic acute stress, on the other hand, can be described as people who are constantly in crisis management. Their lives are in perpetual disarray as "I'm running behind" becomes their mantra. Basically, if something can go wrong in their lives, it will. People who suffer from episodic stress have a hard time facing that they live in a state of chaos. They are quick to blame and often irritable. Often times, pain and discomfort will be the only catalyst for change. Chronic stress is the worst type of stress. This is the constant grinding stress that wears a person down, year after year. This type of stress can stem from past experiences that have been pushed deep inside the psyche of an individual. Problems from childhood that were never dealt with can be found in this category. This type of stress is brought about when a person can't see their way out of a situation so they just give up. Chronic stress is often ignored because it's "the devil you know." It's the comfort zone living that lulls a person to sleep. Some examples of chronic stress might include an abusive relationship or a dead-end job.

Now that we know what stress is and where it comes from, let's concentrate on one of the biggest causes of stress in our lives—the state of uncertainty. Uncertainty can contribute to all three categories of stress. It doesn't matter if your state of uncertainty occurs at home, work, or within a peer group, there is nothing worse than not knowing where you stand. When we suffer from uncertainty, we have the uncanny ability to fill in the blanks of what we don't know. Most of the time, these blanks are riddled with negative thinking and thoughts of lack and limitation. We fill in the blanks based on our perception and opinion of the situation. Most of the time, these opinions and perception are off-base because we are suffering from a state of uncertainty. By that I mean, we aren't sure what someone meant, or how and why someone acted the way they did. Truth of the matter, we have no way of knowing what the other person might've been going through before our "situation" came to light. A good way to stop the downward spiraling madness of perception and opinion is to move into a state of communication. To do this, we must first communicate with ourselves. We have to leave behind all judgments and misconceptions of our perception. We have to move ourselves into a state of openness and understanding because we *don't* know what's going on. Once this self-communication is achieved, we move into communication with the other person. Because we are living in a state of openness and understanding as opposed to stress and reaction, we are providing a fertile ground for positive communication. Communication is always the answer to a state of uncertainty. Through communication, we achieve clarity of a situation that we first "perceived" to be more than it actually was. Has this ever happened to you? You didn't know what was going on, so you filled in the blanks with negative thinking only to later realize you overreacted? When we don't know something, we need to leave it at that. We don't know. Thoughts like: "Did you see the way he/she looked at me? They must not like me. Why did he/she snap at me? Did I do something wrong?" are all examples of filling in the blanks. More often than not, these filled in blanks are wrong. You do not know what the other person was thinking at that very moment. You don't know whether or not his/her spouse just called and chewed them out for something, or their boss was unhappy with them, or whatever. Unless you know for sure, don't "fill in the blanks." Jumping to conclusions or forming an opinion is a waste of time. Resist the desire to fill in the blanks with awfulizing statements. When we repeat these awfulizers in our head, they become a malicious form of self-propaganda, which soon results in self-defeat. *Why not* fill in the blanks with authentic communication and leave the stress behind. If you must fill in the blanks, choose a blank that serves a feeling tone of love and compassion. Tell yourself, "he/she is just having a bad day and this is in no way a reflection of me. I wonder if there's anything I can do for them?"

When I was in college, uncertainty became a way of life because I didn't do my homework. When it was time for an exam, I was simply unprepared. This gives stress an opportunity to thrive. It doesn't take a rocket scientist to discover the best way to pass an exam is to study the material. It wasn't as if the professor was making it a guessing game for us. I could be confident that if it was lectured in class, it would probably appear on the exam. The first step out of uncertainty for me was to go to class. The next step was to study the notes. The final step was to read the text. I wasn't doing any of those things, and so stress was living my life. I was scrambling through a life of uncertainty and I was losing.

Another major contributor to stress is lack of time. We're always on the go, go, go. Essentially, overbooking our lives is a disaster waiting to happen. Without some sort of time management, stress will undoubtedly take over. Fortunately for me, I discovered the importance of time management at the eleventh hour in college. Things were getting dicey as I entered my third semester of being a sophomore. I began the semester with fifteen units, a role in the Shakespeare play *All's Well That Ends Well*, playing trumpet in the jazz band, a full-time party schedule with the fraternity, a part-time job, and a full-time girlfriend. I finished the semester with a whopping three units, and that was for jazz band, the one thing I didn't have to study for. Needless to say, my father was less than thrilled with my performance as he decided to sit me down for a "talk." Talking was something my family excelled at. If we had an issue, we could be confident that it would be worked out one way or another. My parents never glossed over our lives. This is the way it was, and if we didn't like it, well, that was too bad. We were taught to deal with things by way of pushing or pulling it out of ourselves. They made us own up to our actions. I love them for it now, but I didn't back then.

Basically, my parents made sure their kids faced the realities of life. They would sometimes leave us to our misery, but most of the time, the kitchen table was in play. It was at the kitchen table where we would cry, scream, and basically do whatever we needed to do to get the issue out of us, but by the end of the discussion, there was some type of resolution that would be followed by a hug, and we'd move on. Again, I didn't know it at the time, but this type of exercise is such a healthy environment for growth. My family has been a truly amazing influence on my life and I thank everyone for all the lessons, good and bad. There would be no hugs on this day, however. Not even the familiar comfort of the kitchen table was at hand. No, this day was reserved for some tough love, and my life was in desperate need of it.

The cold breeze from my dad's shoulder kissed the air of his office as I entered. Thankfully, my dad never needed to inflict any form of "physical encouragement" upon us, because he was the master of the look. He had this ability to distill an hour-long lecture into one look. That was my father's trademark, but the look on his face that day was one I had never seen before. In fact, there were a lot of things that were different that day. The most surprising was when he handed me a binding contract. He wanted me to sign a binding performance contract. Who gives their son a binding contract? You think I'm kidding?

I didn't know what to do, so I climbed into the role of the victim, which I played quite well. I thought to myself, "how did he know about my grades?" I quickly countered his offensive with my own attack: "You opened my mail?" I was pissed. I did everything to turn the tables on him. He saw me coming a mile away and quickly labeled me a "sanctimonious little shit." I didn't know what that meant, but I knew it wasn't good. Basically, it means smug and self-righteous, and it was perfect because I was trying to turn things around so that I wouldn't be accountable for my actions. I wouldn't stand in the truth because I was so deep in denial that I couldn't see my way out.

In short, my choices were to either sign on the dotted line

or get financially cut off. My books, tuition, half my rent, and a hundred dollars a month for food was the deal offered. Now, even from my immature standpoint at the time, this wasn't a bad deal. If I got cut off, I'd have to get a real job, and I wasn't sure I'd even have time to study. Of course, I wasn't studying *now*, but you get the point. I could've gone to my mother and asked for assistance because mean old Dad was treating me like I was his employee. I imagine if one of his employees had my performance level, they would've been fired on the spot. So, after some tears and more denial, I signed on the dotted line. We shook hands, and from that moment on, I took a vested interest in my life. My father gave me a gift that day. It was at this point of my life where I experienced some much-needed growth. Sure, it was like dragging a dead horse to water, but I finally drank the water. I finally owned up to the fact that my entire semester was based around sorority girls and partying. When I didn't do the homework and would fail a test, I would simply drop the class. When faced with the responsibilities of being a student, I turned the other direction. I preferred the anesthesia of alcohol and road trips to my own education. I wasted my own time.

I discovered the only way for me to combat stress was to be prepared. Stress thrives in an unprepared environment. Before my father's binding contract, I was always playing catch-up. If you play catch-up with your life, you can be sure that stress will find its way in because your whole existence if based on uncertainty. When you spend your time rushing around waiting until the last minute to do something, your body rejects the constant adrenaline rush and something has to give. If you are living a life that is full of stress, you must make changes in order to survive. If ignored, stress will win the battle of life by ending yours. It's time to win back your life one step at a time. Build the house brick by brick, not on a moment's notice. Plan and execute a strategy. Knowing where you stand can give you a sense of calmness, and this calmness gives you the ability to see things more clearly. If you see more clearly, you're more likely to recognize things that have the ability to cause stress in your life. The sooner you can see it, the sooner you can get rid of it. Some like to live in a crisis mode because it gives them the illusion of being alive. In reality, all that occurs is they fill a personal void in their lives with distractions. By living in a mode of crisis, they don't have to deal with the void.

Another thing that can cause stress are the uncontrollable variables in life. Uncontrollable variables are the things that come out of nowhere and slam into our lives with great force. Those pesky things have the knack of popping up out of the blue when you least expect it. They can take on many forms. They can be small things, or large enough to shake you to your knees. These uncontrollable elements have the ability to shoot our stress levels into the red zone—but they have that ability only if you allow them to have it. Your car gets stolen. Stress! You lose your wallet. Stress! You get into an accident. Stress! Your kid comes down with the flu and you can't find a babysitter, so you have to stay home from work despite your need for a full paycheck. Stress! Based on your absence, you get fired. Big stress!

How about this stressful scenario: The latest rainstorm dumps six inches of rain in three hours and your roof caves in, ruining all your new furniture. You just bought the house not three weeks ago and to have this happen is catastrophic. You finally unpacked the last box and everything was in its place. Your housewarming party was scheduled for next week. On top of everything, you discover that your homeowner's insurance policy lapsed because you forgot to pay the bill, which happened because you were stressed out about the move into the new house. If that wasn't bad enough, your spouse is going nuts, and yes, someone will always go nuts in these types of situations. "Oh, my God, how are we going to pay for this? We have no insurance!" Significant levels of stress have kicked in. Through your own reactions and panic, you can't see your way out of the problem. You can't breathe. Suddenly, the walls are closing in.

If we learn to keep it all in some kind of perspective, we'll be fine when uncontrollable variables present themselves. If you are on top of the "given" variables in your day-to-day life, this new problem won't be a piece of cake, but you'll be able to deal with it more efficiently. If you stand in calmness despite the appearances, you're way ahead of the game. Unfortunately, most of us will lay an egg when something like this happens. This is the last thing we should do. Anger and panic only make an already stressful situation worse. With your clear, centered head, you remember what the realtor said on the day you bought the house: "As part of the escrow costs and good faith, your homeowners' insurance is covered for the first month." Well, there you go, problem solved. Bit by bit, the problem is now merely an inconvenience. All that stress and panic was for nothing. Sometimes things aren't always as they appear. Remember when you were first looking at the house and commented on how nice it would be to have a skylight in the living room? Ever wonder if this new problem has anything to do with you "asking" for a new skylight?

### *Chapter 6 Exercise*
## Develop a Stress Balance Sheet!

Make a list of things that cause stress in your life. You might find yourself repeating the "negative influences" list from the last chapter here, and that's okay. Don't hold back and don't edit yourself when drafting a list like this. Lose the fear of anyone seeing this list. This book is your personal work, so get to the heart of it even if your list includes someone you really love.

**Stressors:**

1. _____

2. _____

3. _____

4. _____

5. _____

6. _____

7. _____

Now divide the list into two categories: controllable variables (rent, kids, communication with your lover, school, etc.) and uncontrollable variables (traffic accidents, death of a loved one, etc.). Look at the controllable list and take action. If it's a job you hate, find a new one. Have a big test coming up? Find the time to study. The uncontrollable variables are harder to quantify because they come out of nowhere. There is, however, something you can do to limit the level of stress these uncontrollable variables cause. Determine exactly what your monthly expenses are to survive: rent, water, power, phone, and food. Now add them up and multiply the figure by three. This amount is your safety blanket in case an uncontrollable event slams into your life. If you set aside this amount, and you should, you now have three months to regroup and start over.

# 7

# $\mathcal{L}$ife Is But a Dream

## *If there's no wind, row your own boat.*

What are we if we don't dream? More importantly, what are we if we don't pursue those dreams? Time-clock workers and wage slaves, nothing more. Becoming a slave to money is a horrible existence. When you live your dreams, money simply becomes a by-product. If you aren't willing to take a vested interest in what will happen, what can happen, and what should happen in your life, you're allowing some "thing" to fill in the blanks. *Why not* fill in the blanks of your life with your dream? Do you have a dream? If you do, grab hold of it and never let go. Dive in so deep that the dream becomes your reality. If you won't do it for yourself, who will? Oh, and hold on—it's going to be a bumpy ride.

When you're in the stream of your dreams, nothing can stop you. Henry David Thoreau may have said it best: "If one advances confidently in the direction of their dreams, and endeavors to live the life which they have imagined, they will meet with a success unexpected in common hours." How right he was. When we believe in what we've envisioned, nothing can stop us. We *must* be confident in the decisions we make and *know* this conviction comes from deep inside our soul. Otherwise it's like being on a treadmill, working hard but never really getting anywhere. If we allow uncertainty to enter the equation or have some other chink in our armor, rust will find a way in and we will indeed fail. As soon as we give the negative flow an opportunity to reign, it will soon dominate our thoughts, because giving up is the easy way out. People think success is easy. Success takes work. Success takes conviction in your decisions, so don't waiver no matter what the external circumstances might be. Remember, it's what you do, not what you say. Answer the desire with action, not reaction. "Whatever you can do or dream you can, begin it. Boldness has genius, power, and magic in it." – Johann Wolfgang von Goethe (1749–1832), German poet, playwright, novelist.

Ever wonder why it's so crowded at the bottom of the ladder of success? Giving up is the easy way out and often taken. Personally, the thought of giving up on my dream rattles my soul. I refuse to give up. Unfortunately, the American culture has gravitated to this lazy "what's in it for me" attitude. Not only "what's in it for me," but "what's *free* that's in it for me," has taken our culture by storm. This mental trap doesn't belong anywhere in your new style of thinking. You can't hitchhike your way to your dreams. If you choose to cut corners or cheat your way through life, you're only cheating your true authentic self. Expect to work for what you want. This way, in the end, you'll appreciate your endeavors more as a result of the hard work.

From the moment we learn conceptual thought, we're busy dreaming. We're dreaming about what it would be like to climb a mountain, to fly like a bird, to be a fireman, a police officer, or maybe President of the United States. Do you remember having any of those types of dreams? I often wonder what happens to that style of dreaming as we get older. Does life slap us around so much that we no longer dream about what could be? Suddenly we're satisfied with the quick fix, because we want it now. It's sad, but true. Things don't come fast enough for us. This fast-food mentality is robbing us of our dreams and aspirations. The result is our desire for cushy jobs, which breeds complacency. Complacency breeds mediocrity. Mediocrity breeds boredom. Boredom breeds unhappiness. The spiraling effect can go on forever. *Why not* spin this spiraling effect to work in our favor? *Why not* have one good thing lead to another?

Have you ever heard the story of the phoenix? The phoenix, whose name comes from the Greek word for "brightly colored," is a bird of legend that is said to consume itself by fire after five hundred years of life. The phoenix then rises again, renewed from the ashes. Initially declared sacred by the Egyptian sun god Ra, the phoenix was affiliated with the sun, because it was always driving toward its guiding light. Like the phoenix, we too must arise from the ashes of struggle associated with conceiving and attaining our dreams. In our new style of thinking, we find that strength keeps us moving until the dream becomes a reality. Remember, if you see it, you can become it. Once you've seen it, that vision will forever propel you forward. Say this affirmation aloud: "If I can see it, I can attain it." Say it again, only louder this time: "IF I CAN SEE IT, I CAN ATTAIN IT." Once we "see" our dream, it's virtually impossible to lose sight of it, unless you choose to give up.

Visualize your dreams on a moment-by-moment basis. Stay conscious through the pursuit of your dream—and again, be cautious of dreaming about money. I know some authors will drive home the point of "If you want money, you have to think about money, or dream about money." I'm not here to discount that by any means, because it's true enough. But this book isn't about thinking of money and growing rich financially. We're here to become rich within the very center of our souls. I'll say it again: Financial wealth and other kinds of material abundance are by-products of living your dreams.

The "lottery mentality" has the ability to drive us away from our dreams. Don't wait for the lottery opportunity to knock on your door. Kick the doors of your life wide open and find the way to your dreams. If you don't, who will?

With the help of Madison Avenue and other corporate manipulations, we are told what to eat, what to drink, when to drink it, what to drive, what to dream, and sometimes how to dream. From the time our parents teach us the difference between right and wrong, through years of teachers and superiors "instructing" us on a cornucopia of things to do, we somehow lose sight of our own self-reliance. We forget what *we* want. Remember, you are the authority on what's best for you. You are the author of your life. Listen to what is moving through your heart, and become awake and aware! Focus on your dream and find a way for it to become your reality. Say this aloud: "I am the authority on me! I am the authority on what I choose! I am the authority on me!" Listen to what you want to do. When we listen to ourselves, something happens inside of us that can be compared to a jolt of power. You'll suddenly have a sense of focus and direction that you've never experienced before. Why? Because *you* are driving *you*. You aren't being driven by some "requirement," a company agenda luring you away from your money, or some other external circumstance. You are being driven by a sense of self-knowing, and that's basically what dreaming is all about. Knowing who you are and who you are becoming is the true power of dreams. You see? That's the excitement. *You* are the excitement.

What do you want to be when you grow up? We're growing up every day of our lives, so *why not* become what we dream? Trust in the knowing that you can't go wrong when you listen to your heart. Fulfillment of your heart's innermost desires is paramount to your personal growth. Dream big! Dream tall! Remember the cartoon "Santa Claus is Comin' to

Town"? It's the cartoon where we sang along, "Put one foot in front of the other, and soon you'll be walking across the floor." This is a perfect mantra for any of us. Your dreams shouldn't scare you. They should excite you. It's up to you to get excited about who you want to become. Simply put, move in the direction of your dreams and don't look back. Look forward and fall in love with your life.

### Chapter 7 Exercise
## What's Your Name Again?

**Part 1: VISIONING**

This practice allows the white noise of life to dissipate. I usually choose to do this outdoors when I'm on a mountain bike ride, but you can do this anywhere quiet. Sit in a comfortable position without becoming horizontal. This isn't about the unconsciousness of a nap. Close your eyes and stop thinking about what you did today, what you didn't do, or what you wanted to do. Listen inward. Listen to your heart. To help this transition along, I like to think of a nice, calm lake, nestled high in the Sierra Mountains. The lake water is smooth as glass. I smell the sweetness of pine as the wind lightly kisses the trees overhead. For me, there is calmness about this picture, because this is an exact feeling tone of my heart.

Don't worry if you feel silly the first time you do this. I think everyone does initially, but know the time you're investing is about *you* listening to *your* heart. Feel your heart and where it wants to lead you. Move this vision you've created into the vision of you living your dream. See yourself in your dream. See yourself doing the very thing you dream of. *Do this visioning practice on a daily basis!* If you miss a day, that's okay, but this visioning is key to accessing your dreams and seeing them appear on a moment-by-moment basis.

## Part 2:   EXPRESSION

Resist the time sink activity of watching television and light some candles in your favorite part of the house. Put on your favorite CD and basically create an environment that triggers your vibratory frequency to move into a heart space of love and compassion. Discover a new perspective on your life and feel the freedom in your life. You can do this exercise with someone you love later on, but for right now it's important that you do this alone so make some time for you. Once you've created an environment conducive for creative thought, spend the next hour doing something you like. Read a book. Write in a journal. Draw. Meditate. Paint something. Learn how to do stained glass. Daydream. Whatever you do, make sure it's something that moves your heart.

# 8

## $\mathscr{P}$ractical People
### *– get practical lives.*

Earlier I touched on the fact that our culture has gravitated toward settling for the path of least resistance. People are actually seeking out the cushy jobs. How does the old saying go? "When the going gets tough, the tough get going." Actually, "When the going gets tough, a lot of us become practical" would be applicable these days.

Since we associate risk with living our dreams, a lot of people stop dreaming altogether because of the fear of taking a risk. Living a fear-based life will always prevent you from your desired goal. The only way to actually realize your dreams is to go after them despite your fears. The shortest distance between two points is a direct line. A writer friend of mine on *Law & Order* gave me advice about *re*writing, which essentially *is* writing. He said, "The more waves an idea creates throughout the story, the better your chances are that you've come up with a great idea." This means that there are no quick fixes or paths of least resistance. The better the idea, or the better life we envision, the more waves we'll encounter. "Problems cannot be solved at the same level of awareness that created them." – Albert Einstein (1879–1955). If you're looking for a band-aid to a problem, you're only delaying the pain of the situation. Remember how your mom dealt with band-aids when you were a kid? She'd rip 'em off, fast and furious. Shying away from your vision because of the work associated with the vision is a crime against your dream. Don't be afraid of the risk. Don't be afraid of hard work. Let it rip and watch your dreams become your reality!

We are born with only two fears in life: the fear of falling and the fear of loud noises. Most everything else is learned behavior. The easiest way for us to overcome fear is to face it. Yes, this is easier said than done, but you can't expect your fear to go away unless it's dealt with. Dealing with fear is just like dealing with negative thinking; the sooner you can become aware of it, the sooner you can overcome it. The number-one fear that overshadows all of us is the fear of failing. Nobody wants to fail. But if you focus your drive on "I don't want to fail," you will indeed fail. Why? You're splitting your intentions. It's virtually impossible to *want* and *not want* simultaneously. You can't have it both ways. The universe has no way of deciphering your intentions between "I want" and "I don't want." By saying "I don't want," you're calling that action forth. This is a trap that we fall into from time to time. Affirm in thoughts, words, and actions. "I will succeed," "I will overcome," and "I will." By these positive affirmations, we're reinforcing our desires, not our fears.

Remember, when you trust in who you are, nothing else matters. Simply put, you can't go wrong when you trust in yourself. By saying "I will succeed" and "I will overcome," we're conditioning ourselves to do just that: succeed. Looking further into the trust factor, we learn that the heart of self-esteem is trust. Trust is at the core of passion. Trust is at the core of desire. Trust is at the core of everything. If you don't trust in what you're doing, you'll resort to thoughts that limit the possibilities of your dreams and innermost desires.

Now some might ask, "What about when things go wrong and I fail?" At this point, most would rather curl up and retreat to the cave. But when you've done everything you can to make something happen and you fail, depression and regret is limited, because you at least had the courage to show up. You're proud of yourself for taking the chance and at least giving it a try. Pride is the sanctuary of your heart. Find the power in your failure. As Thomas Alva Edison (1847–1931) once said, "I have not failed. I've just found ten thousand ways that won't work." The biggest mistake anyone can make in life is not giving it a shot. Resist the desire to throw a pity party and dust yourself off. Get back into the game, and start again. This time around, you'll be armed with the knowledge of what went wrong last time around. It's the classic learning curve. Know this, successful people think about success. Failures think about failure. What are you thinking about? What is your attention on? Tom Wilson, the creator of the comic strip Ziggy, once gave these words of wisdom to Ziggy: "You can complain because roses have thorns, or you can rejoice because a thorn bush has roses." Are you taking an active role in the dreams you dream, or are you waiting for your dreams to happen? The world is full of waiters—people waiting for their dreams to come to them. Are you waiting for something to happen or are you taking an active role? Your dreams are waiting for you. Ever ask yourself, "What's my life all about?" or "Does it have meaning?" Are you blasé about your life, answering "I have an okay life" or "I have an okay job"? If this is your answer, then guess what? You're going to have an okay life. There's nothing wrong with an okay life, but don't be surprised or have regret when ten years go by and someone asks "How's it going?" and your reply is, "Everything is *okay*."

Really, do you actually want an okay life? I know I don't. I want to make my life as special and exciting as possible. *Why not?* The only person who can do that for myself is me. Nobody can live my dreams for me. Why would I want them to? It's up to me. How do I do it? It begins with how I see my life. It begins with how I talk to myself in the quiet moments when I'm alone. How are you talking to yourself? I guarantee that if you lead your life by practical decisions, you're going to end up with a practical life. Remember, you get what you put out. Wouldn't you rather have words like amazing, terrific, happy, creative, and inspiring describe who you are or where you are going? It all starts by using a language with a positive tonality. Your vibratory frequency operates at the level in which you desire. Want to be happy? Be it. Now, let's have that friend ask us about our life again. "How are things going?" Your reply might be, "Well, things are *absolutely fantastic!* I just wrote a screenplay and sold it to Warner Brothers." "We just had our second child!" "I've cornered the toy market with this new toy I thought of one day, and now Mattel wants to buy me out for three million dollars!" Okay vs. amazing? Where's the quandary? Having something exciting to say about your own life instead of about the life of someone you emulate is intoxicating. The only way these exciting things will ever happen to *you* is if *you* get excited about *you!* Get excited about your life! *Why not?* If you won't, who will?

Do you see the common thread here? Everything begins and ends with *you!* It's your job to become excited about who you are! Listen to that little voice and change the language that serves your dreams. That voice is a powerful thing, and you should embrace it with positive action. If you aren't hearing that positive voice, it's the same voice that tells you "I can't" do something. It's the same voice that kills your drive. Everyone has an inner voice, what style is yours? How are you talking? Be cognitive of your style, both externally and internally. Become cognitive of your vibration. Are you a dark storm cloud or a shining light? Also, stop thinking the world owes you something because it doesn't. Nobody owes you a thing. Your parents don't. Your job doesn't. Your boss doesn't. Your God doesn't. Not even your wife, husband, or lover. If you want to feel like somebody owes you something, take a look in the mirror. That's the person who owes you something. You owe it to yourself to become what you dream about. Stop the blame game and get busy. Your life is waiting. Stop dreaming about the life that seems so far away and start living it today. It's yours for the taking. All too often we complain about what we didn't get, what we should've gotten, or what we really deserved. These kinds of thoughts only breed resentment, and you know what that breeds—a downward spiral into the depths of nothingness.

So now you've decided to do something about your dreams, but you aren't sure about diving into the deep end just yet. You have thoughts like "Maybe I'll do it part time. Maybe I'll do it on the weekends." Don't play that game either. Kick "maybe" to the curb with ego and negativity. Nothing good comes from playing it safe. You want your dreams? Get ready to dive in, because this is your life you're talking about and you don't have time to be blasé. Find the excitement in pushing the envelope. Don't be practical when you're looking at your dreams. Think big. Dream big. Dream tall. Never take second place with a smile. Swing for the fences and you might hit the ball. If you don't have a bat in your hands, you're surely to miss the ball entirely. *Why not* give your dreams a shot? Who knows, lightning could strike. "It's kind of fun to do the impossible." – Walt Disney (1901–1966).

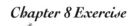

## *Chapter 8 Exercise*
## Doing the "Three-Step Boogie"

Fear, doubt, and worry are misguided thoughts which are strengthened by what we don't know, or what we "think" we might know. In this exercise, you're going to keep track of your negative thoughts, or as I like to call them, your "boogie man." Some boogie man examples might be: "How could I be so stupid. I'm fat. I'm not pretty. That was a stupid thing to say. I can't do this, or I can't do that." Throughout the day, learn to recognize and put a net over the boogie man by practicing three small steps known as the "Boo-Be-Gone."

### Step 1:   "BOO"
When you discover a boogie man, quickly write it down on a piece of paper. It doesn't matter where you are, or what you're doing. If you're at a party, excuse yourself, go to the bathroom, and write it down. Write it on a gum wrapper if you have to, but write it down.

### Step 2:   "BE"
Move into a state of beingness (being true to who you are and who you want to become) by practicing positive affirmations that support the "**I AM**," "**I WILL**," and "**I CAN**" principles. Some examples might be: "**I AM** pretty," "**I WILL** get the job," or "**I CAN** do this."

### Step 3:   "GONE"
Strike through the self-defeating statement and flush it. Flush the negativity away and move on with strength, courage, and wisdom.

# 9

## "I'm Not Creative"

### *An exercise in trust*

Anything starting with "I'm not" is a statement that will kill your motivation. "I'm not" should be lost from your vocabulary. Go ahead, kick it to the curb so ego has some company. Anything you say that limits you will undoubtedly defeat you. All we have to do is replace "I'm not" with "I am." "I'm not creative" is now "I am creative." "Very few people do anything creative after the age of 35. The reason is that very few people do anything creative before the age of 35." – Joel Hildebrand (1881–1983), chemistry professor.

Somehow, people manage to negatively condition themselves to think that creativity is unattainable for them because they don't play an instrument or know how to paint. To be truly creative, you have to let go of your inhibitions and trust. Some might call this ability self-confidence, but in reality it's just a sense of knowing that you have with yourself. This knowing is trust. Somehow, this "I'm not creative" phrase has become a mantra in our society. We have seen a shift from people with low self-esteem to people with no self-esteem. We're choking on information and propaganda, but starving for direction and drive. Become your own inspiration by trusting in yourself. When someone asked Francois-Auguste Rodin (1840–1917) how he managed to create such remarkable statues, he simply replied: "I choose a block of marble and chop off whatever I don't need." Simply put, he just does it.

He doesn't worry about what others might think of what he's doing or what he's creating. The finished product is a by-product of his trust.

The single thing that separates those who are creative from those who claim they *aren't* creative is that creative people act without fear, doubt, or worry of what someone might think. That's the only difference. What does it really mean to be creative to you? Would you consider a painter creative? How about a writer? What about someone who's well versed in woodworking, crafts, or even music? Please remember that creativity isn't limited to the arts, because everyone has the ability to be creative. Creativity means trusting your "out of the box" thinking and putting those thoughts into action. Have you ever seen the car commercial that proclaims "Color outside the lines"? From the earliest stages of childhood, we are told if we color outside the lines in our coloring book, we're "doing it wrong." We can recognize this as a beginning of societal conformity, or "fitting in." We're told how to hold the crayon, and sometimes what colors to use. If my niece Tyler Marie wants to color a tree blue, then I say let her, because that's the crux of creativity. What's wrong with a blue tree? Why aren't we given the green light to let the crayon flow where it wants? Why is it considered "wrong" to color a blue tree? If an artist paints a blue tree, he's either labeled a visionary artist or color-blind nut job. Exactly who decides the right and wrong when personal expression is at hand? Having the courage to make your thoughts become reality is the very heart of creative expression. Trusting in your decisions—now that's creativity. "Creativity is allowing oneself to make mistakes. Art is knowing which ones to keep." Scott Adams, author/illustrator *The Dilbert Principle.*

Have you ever seen the major league baseball player Hideo Nomo pitch a game? This is the Japanese wonder boy who took the baseball world by storm back in the 1995 season pitching for the L.A. Dodgers. He's got the most unorthodox pitching style of anyone who's ever played the game. His coaches in Japan tried to "teach" him how to pitch correctly when he was young player. They told him, "Nobody pitches like that." He told them, "This is the way I pitch." He ignored their criticism, and they finally left him alone because he was getting the desired results. If it weren't for my high school classmate Greg Maddux (5-time Cy Young award winner for the Atlanta Braves), Hideo Nomo probably would have won the National League Cy Young award that year as a rookie. I often wonder how those criticizing coaches feel now. I love the fact that this guy held true to his own style and remained authentic to his heart. This is a great example for all of us. It's important to trust in who you are. It's important to resist the pressure of other people's opinions. Some of the greatest inventors bucked the status quo and looked to the horizon with a curious eye. Conforming yourself to the status quo will garnish you the status quo. Run away from societal pressures to "fit in" and embrace original thought.

My brother Gary is extremely gifted in creative expression, and his children are no different. Riley and Carley Mae continue to amaze me with the way they trust in their thoughts and vision of what could be. For example, Carley Mae wrote the following poem when she was seven years old:

**LOVE IS PINK**
*It sounds like a water fall.*
*It smells like honeysuckles.*
*It tastes like sugar cookies,*
*and it looks like flowers in the sun.*

This is an amazing piece of expression when we look at her age. Imagine that coming from a seven-year-old girl. As for Riley, not only is he talented in music, but some of his best artwork has been in a wild, abstract form. His pen flows without fear of "doing it wrong." If my brother stood over their shoulders and told them not to color a blue tree, would we get to appreciate their work? No, we'd get the confines of conformity. I see the same creative freedom with my sister Stacey's children. My niece Tyler Marie and nephew Matthew do whatever they "feel" when expression is concerned, sometimes to Stacey's dismay. Some might see their actions as rebellious, but a lot of the time creative expression is at the heart of their actions. From time to time, I get artwork postcards from both of them. Their work is also free and expressive, and I love them for it.

The beauty about children is that they aren't really concerned with what other people think of their work. Unless directed on how to color a tree, we can be sure that children will color outside the lines. Now, why can't we take this freedom of expression into our adult lives? Why do we feel the need to be validated by someone else's opinion? In the entertainment industry, it's appreciation by committee. Studio executives shy away from original work until it becomes successful. Why do you think we keep seeing the same kind of movies with the same actors, over and over? Studio executives buy into the fear that people won't come to something new and different, so they green-light the same regurgitated ideas: *Die Hard* meets *Charlie's Angels*. *Star Wars* meets *The Lord of the Rings*. Imagine if Hollywood ever embraced something we've never seen before. The story behind the successful movie, *My Big Fat Greek Wedding* is a perfect example. Every studio passed on the picture saying it was too small. The project developed after actor Tom Hanks and his wife, Rita Wilson, who is Greek-American, saw Nia Vardalos' Los Angeles stage play in 1998. They liked it so much that Hanks purchased the rights through his production company, Playtone Co., and agreed to let Vardalos adapt the story and take the starring role. To date, the film has made over $200,000,000 at the box office. Now that the film is a huge success, you can be confident studio executives are in development meetings asking, "Do you have anything like *My Big Fat Greek Wedding*?"

Usually, when it's time to think freely, we shut down and wait for instructions because that's what we've been taught; information in, information out. Throughout school, we're taught to memorize a list of words or some new math formula, and then regurgitate the information for an exam. For some reason, we're cut off from free thinking by this memorization discipline. I'd say the only place in our school system where you find a totally free-flowing approach is in a theater arts class for an impromptu scene study, creative writing, or other liberal arts classes. Shouldn't creativity and free thinking be an integral part of every class? Shouldn't creativity and free thinking be an integral part of our daily lives? We need to teach ourselves to break down the barriers of "fitting in" by embracing the unknown. We need to teach ourselves to color outside the lines whenever possible. We need to teach our minds to ask "*Why not?*" What's the worst thing that could happen? You don't win the national conformity coloring contest? I'm okay with that. Are you? How are you coloring your life? Are you breaking free from the desire to "fit in?" *Why not* start today?

### Chapter 9 Exercise
### Yes, I AM creative!

This should be fun. Get yourself a piece of paper and a pen. No pencils and no erasers allowed for this exercise. Write down your favorite number on a blank piece of paper. Write it nice and big. I'm going to use the number 7 for our illustration because I love it so much. What you're about to do is an exercise in trust. There's only one rule we have for this exercise: no "thing" is wrong.

Here we have our number, nothing fancy or elaborate. It's just the basic number. Now I want you to take your pen and block the number.

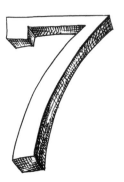

Now we continue by adding some shading to the number. A couple of lines here a couple of lines there, and we can see our number evolving into something with more style. It's something more than we had before. This is a good way of looking at how the process of creativity really works. The same goes for writing. The same goes for any "thing" in our lives, including ourselves. Do you have any idea how many drafts will take place before someone like John Grisham lets go of a novel? Do you know how many drafts I've written on this book? Too many to list, but the exciting thing about creativity is that it's always a work in progress. You never finish, you just find a place to stop.

During this work in progress, you find that something distracted you from your exercise and the pen just went too far right when you added the shading. Some times the pen has a mind of its own. When this happens, some of us will look at it and think it's ruined. No, no, no. Let's allow this "mistake" to show us the road we haven't thought of until now. Let go of the steering wheel and give into the process, because something is trying to come out of you.

Creativity works through our hearts and not through our minds. My good friends Dr. Michael Beckwith and Dr. Rickie Byars-Beckwith (www.rickiebyars.com) wrote a song titled, "I Release and I Let Go." What a truly insightful notion. "I release and I let go." The title of the song is perfect for this example. You can find more of their music at www.rickiebyars.com or www.agapelive.com. I love that song and I love them for their constant vision and support. The feeling tone behind "I release and I let go" is exactly how creativity should feel: releasing what you already know and letting go of inhibitions to discover something you might never have thought about. The illustration would have never become what it is now unless we recognized the "mistake" as a new opportunity. The illustration would have never become what it is now unless we realized that there are no mistakes, only variations of perception.

If we ask an artist to offer some insight on their latest painting, they will confess that it has taken on a shape of its own since its conception. Unless they are working on assignment and need to deliver exactly what was discussed, they are constantly changing the piece and allowing it to unfold in its own divine way. We can look at our lives this way. "Mistakes" are opportunities for us to discover something that we hadn't thought of. Creativity is trust. If we can't trust ourselves, then how do we expect trust from other people? Trust somewhere. Go for it. Dream big. Dream tall. *Why not?*

# Lights! Ideas! Action!

## *Your life is waiting!*

Taking the creativity issue further, let's consider the concept of ideas. In order to do that, we must first reiterate the ongoing theme of trust. Just because someone tells you no, that doesn't mean your idea or vision should cease to exist. You have to trust in the idea with everything, because dream implementation doesn't happen overnight. It's a long and winding road, so buckle up with trust.

Have you ever seen the late-night infomercials with Jay "The Juiceman" Kordich? He's the guy who made millions with his juicer, and he'll be making millions long after he's passed on. All this from a juicer, you say? No, all this from an idea. People have been making juicers for years, so why did Jay revolutionize the market with his Juiceman Juicer? He raised the bar on expectations, and now everyone else is running to catch up.

Everything began in the late 1940s when Jay was told he was suffering from toxicity by his doctor. He began to think of ways to alleviate the condition through dietary means. Knowing the benefits of fruits and vegetables, Jay thought about juice therapy for his problem. The juicers on the market all lacked the power he imagined a juicer should have. Did he give up on his idea? No, he envisioned a revolutionary juicer that would change the industry. It wasn't an ordinary juicer, but a juicer that would do what others haven't been able to do:

separate the pulp from the juice without bogging down. He finally sold a company on the idea, and they built the machine. Unfortunately, the company made a juicer that wasn't what Jay had wanted. Looking for ways to save money, they had cut corners with the motor. Frustrated at the setback, Jay held onto his dream and pressed on.

With the help of an inventor, Jay developed his dream juicer and went broke. They still had a problem with the motor, but Jay was out of money. Did he give up? No, he pressed on and finally found someone to make the necessary improvements to the motor. In less than a year's time, he became a multi-millionaire. He trusted in his idea even when other's told him it was a waste of time and money. He put an idea into action and refused to listen to all the negative "things" that told him he couldn't do it. He pressed forward by telling himself, "I know this will happen." He had the light in his heart that made him know his idea was good. He listened to his heart and passion carried him through. Passion is the key for any realization of dreams. Personally, I love the concept of putting ideas into action. It doesn't matter what the idea is, I just love it when I see people executing their innermost desires.

Putting ideas into action can be one of the hardest things to execute. We often hear people say, "Oh, I thought of that before," or "Everyone knew that." The next time you hear someone say that about someone else's idea, ask them, or better yet, ask yourself, what happened to the idea when you thought about it? What did you do about it? Nothing happened, because we didn't think it was good enough to fly. Wouldn't that burn our egos if we had an idea and someone beat us to the punch and sold the idea to a large corporation? That's what inventors have over everyone else. They get the idea and actually *do* something about it. They don't talk about it, they *do* it. That's it, they *just do it!* Sound familiar? Imagine if Debbie Fields had listened to the following response to her idea for a cookie store: "A cookie store is a bad idea. Besides, the market research reports say America likes crispy cookies, not soft and chewy cookies like you make."

Never allow fear, doubt or worry of the unknown stop you from your ideas. Living is, truly believing in the impossible. When Alexander Graham Bell invented the telephone, an Executive at Western Union had the following to say in a company memo in 1876: "This 'telephone' has too many shortcomings to be seriously considered a means of communication. This device is inherently of no value to us." Imagine if Alexander had thought this way of his idea. Hold true and love your ideas. Love your desires. This book is based on one thing and one thing only: love. It's an explanation of how many ways we can see it, and how many different ways can we feel it. Can you be the first to love? More often than not, people practice reciprocating love if they even love at all. Very rarely will someone love first unless they know the person. Why? Most people are uncomfortable taking the first step because it involves putting ourselves out there for rejection. We aren't sure what's going to happen, so we choose to do nothing. *Why not* be the one to take the first step? *Why not* be the first to express love? *Why not* live in the land of possibilities? Who knows, you just might meet someone who will change your life forever.

Have you ever heard of the guy who came up with an idea for an overnight mail service? He was a Yale management student named Frederick Smith. Fred came up with the idea as an assignment for his senior economics paper. The topic of his paper was a business that offered overnight mail service. Sounds brilliant, right? Let's say you had an aunt who lived in Florida. Auntie wakes up on Monday and realizes that it's your birthday on Tuesday. Fredrick Smith's company would deliver the package overnight in time for the celebration. The great thing about his idea is that he guaranteed his service. Auntie would have to pay a little extra money in postage, and the item would be guaranteed to make it there in time. Not only that, if you pay a little more, you can have it there before ten o'clock the next morning. Brilliant concept, right? Do you have any idea what grade the professor gave Fred for this idea? The professor wrote, "The concept is interesting and well-formed, but in order to earn better than a 'C' the idea must be feasible."

Here's a kid with a radical idea for the "can't wait" culture we're living in, and he's given a C–. Fred moved past the block of someone else's perception and put his ideas into action. After graduation, Fred kept with it and soon found someone to believe in the idea, and Federal Express was born. Today FedEx is a worldwide multibillion-dollar company that has revolutionized the way we send packages. I wonder how the professor feels now. I wish I woulda, I sure coulda, yep, I probably shoulda. Those three words can never enter your consciousness. *Never!* They only lead to regret. See past the immediate, and recognize where the regrets are born. Put your idea into action.

When Mark Victor Hansen wanted to publish *Chicken Soup for the Soul,* everyone they approached said the book was too soft and nobody would buy it. Did Mark and his co-author, Jack Caulfield, give up? Of course you know they didn't, but what Mark and Jack did was push through by saying "next." If someone said no, they would say "next." Instead of kicking a rock around because of the rejection, they saw through the seeming block by focusing their attention on their dream. They had a vision. This is exactly what we have to do with our dreams. We have to see what we dream. We have to live what we dream. Who wants to kick a rock around? I know I don't and I'm guessing you don't either. When the Beatles sent in their demo tape to the Decca Recording Company in 1962, an executive commented: "We don't like their sound, and guitar music is on the way out." The execution of your desire is going to be work, but don't give up despite what someone might say. You have to trust in your vision and fill yourself with an undeniable passion. You will get rejected. You will be tested, so brace yourself for the journey. Brace yourself with trust and *see* your dream becoming a reality. If you don't see it, who will?

Ideas come in all sorts of shapes and sizes. You never know when a great idea might come your way so be prepared. What makes the ideas listed above different from everyone else's? These are examples of ideas that were put into action. The creators of the ideas put themselves in a place of trust. They put themselves in a place where thinking outside the box was an everyday occurrence. Sounds simple, don't you think? It sounds so simple that we have to ask ourselves, "Why aren't more people doing it?" The answer goes back to that four-letter word, *risk.* For some reason, whenever risk is attached, we slip into vapor lock. In reality, risk should be an exciting thing for us to embrace. Risk is a word that conjures up only one word for me: opportunity. We'll go into risk a bit more in a later chapter, but remember, nothing ventured, nothing gained. Risk is an important part of the equation. If you want to be great, you have to learn to embrace risk. You have to embrace the unknown with trust in yourself. When you trust in yourself, you learn how to *live* your ideas. It's a trickle-down effect that starts with the only ingredient needed for success: *you.* Everything starts with *you.* You are the inventor of yourself. *Why not* invent someone excellent? Invent someone brilliant! Invent someone exciting! Invent someone who leads with love in their heart! *Why not* dream the ultimate you? Your possibilities are endless. You possibilities are limited to your imagination. If you can see it, you can be it.

### *Chapter 10 Exercise*
### Put It on Paper!

Ever wonder how many thoughts travel through our minds in a single day? A single hour? Don't fall into the "I'll remember that" trap. If you were single and you met someone you really liked, would you write their phone number on a piece of paper, or would you tell yourself "I'll remember that"? Think of the regret you'd have if you forgot their number. They could have been the love of your life, and you didn't write it down? Treat your thoughts, dreams, and aspirations with respect. Write them down and put your ideas into action.

For this exercise you're going to need to buy a notebook or journal of some kind. If you can't see yourself carrying around a journal wherever you go, I suggest buying three; one for your office, one for your nightstand, and one for your car. You can find these small notebooks at your local bookstore in the journal section. Artist sketchbooks are great and less expensive than a book store journal so find something that works for you. You're going to start a journal of your life experiences. Rule #1 is to never fear the blank page. Don't sit there and contemplate too long about what you're going to write. Just do it. Write. Let it come out. The blank page can be a metaphor for the life you dream. What would you like to fill the page with?

When you first start out, you'll find yourself "documenting" your life, and that's okay. That's a start. Remember, we're starting somewhere, and that somewhere is nowhere near the top of execution. Right now it's moving into practice. Practice makes perfect. The more you do it, the more you'll learn to trust your ideas, thoughts, and actions—and more importantly, the more you'll learn to trust yourself. Never be caught without something to write in. You never know when a piece of brilliance might want to come through you, so be prepared.

# 11

## $\mathcal{P}$ut Another Log On the Fire
### *What are you waiting for?*

While you're in pursuit of your dreams, you need to keep busy with other things. By discovering other passions, you are bettering your chances of "it" happening in your life. The "it" I'm referring to is the ever-elusive "big break" that everyone seems to wait for. Don't be a "waiter," waiting for the world to come to your door, serve yourself. You see, by expanding and unfolding into the "more" we often dream about, we're allowing the possibility of greatness to enter our lives. For example, I'm writing this book, learning the piano, finishing a screenplay, staying involved with my church and, oh yeah, I'm securing five million dollars for a script I recently optioned.

One of the main reasons we're here on this planet is so that we can unleash our talents by exploring self-expression. If you can agree with that, then you should also agree that it is your responsibility to pursue most everything you dream about. Of course, you can't do everything, but that doesn't mean you should stop exploring the unknown. You never know where the fish are going to bite, so keep yourself busy. You can't expect the fish to bite on your hook if you don't even have a line in the water. Are you watching your life away in front of the TV every night? Consider a change of pace. Listen to music. Write. Go on a hike after work or learn a new hobby. Grab your lover and dance the night away right there in your living room. Do something, but stay busy because you never know what might happen during the adventure.

Let's say I'm writing a children's adventure movie set in a small town in Washington. At the same time, I might be writing a TV pilot script for a series modeled loosely after one of my all-time favorite TV shows, *Mission Impossible*. Just for fun, let's say I was taking an art class at UCLA Extension. Imagine, if you will, fate stepping in while I was at class one night. Maybe my wife-to-be sits next to me, and we begin the first conversation of a lifelong friendship. Or maybe the teacher is married to an executive at Universal Pictures who recently confessed that he wanted to do a show modeled on *Mission Impossible*. One can never anticipate these types of examples, but it sure is funny how life has a way of working out in our favor if we're open to it. Make yourself available, because you never know—lightning could strike.

Did you know John Philip Souza spent most of his life dreaming about writing a great waltz? Every single time he sat down to write, he began with the rhythm of a waltz in mind. As we know, he's known as the king of the march, but every one of his songs first began as a waltz. Imagine if he resisted the idea of playing the songs as marches. Imagine all the great music we would have missed out on because Souza chose to stifle his creativity and not go with the flow. Maybe that was his path to greatness. Maybe he had to write the waltz to get to the march. Things have a way of working together in harmony.

One Sunday morning in July, I met a guy by the name of John "the silver man." John sold silver jewelry at the Rose Bowl swap meet in Pasadena, California. John was very original and very much in tune with who he was and the dreams he had. You see, he was at the Rose Bowl to make money so he could open a retail jewelry shop on Melrose Avenue. For fun,

John used to tie-dye some of his clothes. You could always spot John with some new piece of work draped around him. He loved to call these garments his "walking canvas," and people always commented on them. One shirt in particular changed his life.

It was a silk shirt tie-dyed in random colors. The shirt turned out to be pretty cool, and whenever he wore it, people wanted to know where he got it. For kicks, he took the shirt to a high-dollar, culturally hip store, which has locations in Beverly Hills, Santa Monica, and New York, to see if they liked it as well. The Santa Monica store manager loved it so much that she ordered five for the store. In less than three days, the shirts sold out. The store manager quickly called John and ordered fifty more. John felt a bit overwhelmed, but the money was right and this put him that much closer to opening the jewelry shop on Melrose. While he was accepting his check for the fifty new shirts, the store manager told him that she spoke with the regional sales manager, and they had decided to order his shirts for all of their stores, including the stores in New York. He would need to supply close to one thousand shirts. On top of that, they wanted to find out about John's spring line and other ideas he had about upcoming trends. They thought John was some hotshot designer. When the store manager asked about his spring line, he thought, "Oh no, I don't have a spring line!" Guess what? He does now.

John was at first ambushed by thoughts of lack and limitation, but in reality, all he needed was a new way of seeing himself. In his mind, he was John "the silver man" who wanted to open a jewelry shop on Melrose. He wasn't a clothing designer, let alone a cutting-edge trendsetter. John made a shirt that he thought was cool and it turned out that other people thought the same way. Isn't that what trendsetting is—doing something different? Doing something that isn't popular *is* trend-setting. Simply put, trendsetting is taking risks and embracing the unknown. Sound familiar? Make your own trend by trusting in who you already are! Become open and available for great things in your life by diversifying your talents. Try new things. Explore the unknown with passion. Do as much as you can handle. Diversify. Never put all your eggs in one basket. Feed your mind. Become a sponge for knowledge. Never think you've reached the end of learning just because you're out of school. Life is one big university. Soak it up. *Why not* do everything on your list of dreams? Take comfort in knowing that your life isn't some dress rehearsal. This is it. This is life, right here, right now. "The bravest are surely those who have the clearest vision of what is before them, glory and danger alike, and yet notwithstanding go out to meet it." – Thucydides (about 471–400 BC).

### *Chapter 11 Exercise*
### Stoke Your Own Fire!

Write down seven things you want to do in your lifetime. What is your dream of dreams? Have fun writing this list. Dream big, dream tall, and don't think of your dreams as being small. Is there a book inside of you? Write it. Looking for independence? Become a small-business owner. Still talking about riding your motorcycle up the California coast? Stop dreaming about your life and start living it. Dive in!

## My Lifetime To-Do List:

1. _____

2. _____

3. _____

4. _____

5. _____

6. _____

7. _____

## 12

# New Year's Resolutions
## *Change is NOW!*

Who started this silly custom? We indulge in excessive living all year, and then cap it off with the forbidden fudge, fat-filled cookies, and hangovers of the holidays. Then, as the fashion magazines and TV sell us on unrealistic views of our bodies, we experience guilt (which is another great waste of time) and develop a new enthusiasm that we think will help us solve the problem. "We must become the change we want to see." – Mahatma Gandhi (1869–1948).

Why do we wait for a predetermined time of year to make positive inroads in our own lives? Every year after Christmas, coffee talk and water cooler meetings spark up around the country as people discuss the upcoming year. "So, what are your New Year's resolutions? What are you giving up?" Answers like "lose weight," "save money," "find a new job," "be nice," "control my anger" and "join a gym—again" are only a few examples of this crazy tradition. Resist the urge to wait for your life and take control today. You aren't sure where to begin? Well, let's look at the definition of a word that exemplifies a place for us to begin. *Webster's Dictionary* lists the following definitions for "gravitate": *1. To move under the force of gravity. 2. To be drawn as if by an irresistible force.* This is precisely how we need to be when pursuing our dreams. We need to be drawn by an irresistible force. The only way this irresistible force can happen in your life is if your heart is in play. If your dream is surrounded by ego, desire for money, or other accumulation pitfalls, you won't feel the pull that carries you through the dark times. You won't feel it because it's not connected to your soul. It's not an authentic part of you. Your soul is everything when your dreams are concerned. Without it, you're only spinning your wheels. Each day, you must gravitate toward your authentic dreams. If you set a goal, you have to trust it. You have to own it. You have to be it. Remember, there's no working at it, either. Be it. Be the very thing you desire. Immaculate conception doesn't happen. Does it ever? This journey can be hard, but you've got no other choice. Your heart is calling.

Have you ever noticed how some people choose to run off at the mouth when they are pursuing their goals? I've done it and I'm sure you've done it as well. Something about this practice worries me. On the one hand it's good to tell everyone, because they will hold us accountable for the dream. On the other hand, it's good to shut up and focus. Don't talk about it, *just do it.* Don't let the cat out of the bag before the cat has had a chance to meow. The problem with telling everyone, like most New Year's resolutions, is that if we fail, our self-esteem takes a big hit and we kick a rock around for weeks. We listen to negative thoughts like "Everyone knows I failed" and "I look like a big dummy." If you know that those thoughts will occur, don't tell anyone about your desire. Keep the secret and *just do it.*

Remember the voice inside your head the next time failure presents itself in your life. Do you have self-defeating thoughts, or are you using the experience to forever propel you forward? Failure is an opportunity. "We are not retreating— we are moving in another direction." – General Douglas MacArthur (1880–1964). Failure is an opportunity to see things in a new light or give us a new direction in which to move.

We have an opportunity to use the failure to strengthen ourselves. *Why not* turn it around and use it to power us forward? Look on the brighter side of things. Better yet, how about looking on the brighter side of things before you are forced to? How we deal with failure is important, because failure is not only an opportunity, it is a lesson. The failure is there for us to recognize something about ourselves. Remember, there are no mistakes. It is up to you to find the lesson in the failure that presents itself. Could you have planned better? Could you have had more financing? Could you have joined forces with someone and formed a strategic alliance? The list of possibilities can go on forever. Find the lesson and use it to your advantage. Don't use the situation as a roadblock, use it as a launching pad to move in another direction.

For me, it's been kind of fun to keep this book a secret. I'm walking around with this smile inside of me that I can't wait to share. This book is a smile from my heart to my family, friends, and the friends and family I have yet to meet. If someone responds to it, I know it's because I've reached their heart. At the end of the day, it really doesn't matter if this book is published by a major publisher or not. It doesn't matter if I sell twenty thousand copies or I sell two hundred thousand copies. Sales of the book are merely a by-product of answering the authentic call of my heart. When you follow your heart, the universe will conspire in your favor and great things will indeed happen. "I find the harder I work, the more luck I seem to have." – Thomas Jefferson (1743–1846).

On the other hand, if your goal is something you need help with, such as kicking the habit of any kind, you need to tell someone. You need support for these sorts of things. Tell your spouse, your family, your friends, or your roommates— hell, tell your dog if you think it might do any good. You see, by doing this, you're broadening your support base. Your friends and family can support you with friendly reminders when and if you start to slip. They also won't be offering up any of the "forbidden fruit," because they know you're trying to quit. Please, don't beat yourself up emotionally if you do indeed slip. Don't say, "well, I've blown it now, what's the use, I'll give up entirely." Everyone falls off the horse from time to time, and that's okay. What's important about falling off the horse is how you dust yourself off. Remember, giving up is the easy way out. Don't wait for tomorrow or some other pre-determined date to make changes in your life. If you want a new you, embrace a new you. If you want a new life, embrace a new life. Embrace your desires right now and make it happen. *Why not?*

### Chapter 12 Exercise
### Love Note Affirmations!

Are you beginning to feel the inherent power from statements like, "I am talented," "I love who I am and where I am going," "Good things will happen for me," "I will succeed in my profession," "I am the right person for the job." and "I believe and trust in myself?" Your exercise for this chapter is to write down your affirmations on 3" × 5" index cards. These are the love notes of your life. These are love notes from *yourself* to *yourself.* Place your love notes in areas of high visual traffic. Tape one to the bathroom mirror. Tape one to the dashboard in your car. Tape one to the inside jacket of your daily calendar. Tape one to your computer monitor. Lose the fear of having others see your love notes. Who knows, maybe your love note will cause someone to capture their own dream. If you can't move past this fear, then don't stop—just improvise. Make up some sort of code that only you would know; for example, WWJD (*What Would Jesus Do*) is a good one. When I was in junior high school, my mother and I used, "Did I tell you today?" This was our way of saying *I love you* during a time in my life where talking about love wasn't "cool." We found a way around the peer pressure. I love it because that saying is still with us today. Remember, what other people think of you is none of your business. This is for your benefit, so lose the fear and dive in.

# 13

# Yesterday

## Leave your troubles, come on, be happy!

For some reason we are completely predictable in the way we deal with yesterday or something that *has* already happened. We constantly base today, or even tomorrow, on how yesterday went. It's time to leave your troubles behind. Today is right now! Sure, learn from your past, but don't continue to relive it. Today is the only day you have. Yesterday is gone and tomorrow is only a thought. The only thing you can know for sure is right now. Today is *right now!* "Worrying is wasting today's time cluttering up tomorrow's opportunities with yesterday's troubles" – Anonymous.

If we receive each day as a gift from God, why do we attach "conditions" based on past occurrences? We have the absolute power on how we approach the day, so *why not* approach it with greatness in mind? Hear that? *You* have the power to choose your vibration! Are you choosing joy, happiness, creativity, bliss, and love? Your vibration for each day doesn't come from some external "thing" or past experience, it comes from within who you are! Sure, some days are challenging, but as we now know, these challenges are hidden opportunities, regardless of how they appear. Move into an authentic feeling tone that serves *right now* because that is your gift from your God—right now!

Remember the saying, "It isn't as bad as it seems"? Something happened to me a few weeks ago that might bring this saying into focus. I had just bought a brand-new car. My neighbor Danny and I were washing our cars in the alley one Saturday morning. I had a busy day, but I knew if I didn't wash the car today, my schedule wouldn't allow it during the week. I finished first and wanted to pull my car back into the garage. Well, Danny had just pulled his brand-new BMW M3 closer to my garage so he could finish dressing the tires. This meant I had to back up before pulling into my garage. In the process, I hit the telephone pole. I jumped out to discover a huge black scratch on the edge of the bumper. Measuring about six inches high and three inches long, the scratch was a sight to see. The pole took the paint right off and I could see the black plastic of the bumper. I knew this sort of scratch meant buying a whole new bumper. Once that plastic is scratched, it's difficult to paint over and match the rest of the car. I knew this because I was rear-ended by some lady on the 405 in my old car that produced a scratch just like the one I was seeing. I wasn't happy.

The first thing that came to mind was how close Danny's car was to mine. If he hadn't pulled up and hogged all the room, I wouldn't have needed to back up. Immediately I was looking for someone to blame, when it was clearly my fault. After the initial anger subsided, I got some rubbing compound to see how bad the scratch actually was. Would you be amazed if I told you that the entire scratch came off? I mistook the black tar from the telephone pole as being the black plastic underneath the paint on my bumper. Think of all that time I wasted with reactive anger because I based what was happening right now on some past experience. I felt so foolish, but the lesson was clear.

We can look at each day as a blank, white canvas. This canvas is your life. You have the power to decide what you want to paint. I had the power of deciding how I was going to deal with the appearance of a giant scratch on my bumper. I lost sight of right now and based the situation on a past experience when in reality the situation wasn't as bad as I assumed it to be. You see, I chose to paint a cloudy day when I backed into the telephone pole. The moment it happened, it was up to me and I chose the dark storm clouds of reaction. I moved out of my bliss and into the land of appearances, basing my *right now* on something that happened with my old car. That situation had nothing to do with this situation. They are mutually exclusive of one another.

The white canvas of our day is ours to do with as we see fit. *Why not* paint something great? *Why not* paint something amazing? Why set out to have a bad day by worrying about yesterday's appearances? *Why not* begin each day in a state of bliss? *Why not* begin each day embraced in a state of love? If you want gloom and doom, watch the "Team Coverage" of "Breaking News," but don't make your whole life the five o'clock news. More importantly, don't buy into the land of appearances, because what you see isn't always what you get.

As you leave yesterday behind, you're allowing yourself to move into the state of now. You're allowing yourself to move into a state of knowing that you can do with as *you* see fit. *Why not* please yourself and listen to your heart by moving into a heart space that is wide open? Is there anything better than that? Is there anything better than love? *Why not* make each day the very best it can be? Remember, you have the absolute power to paint yourself a beautiful life.

Okay, I know this plan is unnerving for some and you want to ask the question: What about when a day gets really bad, or something really awful happens? Sure, this happens. After all, this is life, right? Life is unpredictable, and sometimes "shit happens," but that doesn't mean you have to jump into it. Never allow some "thing" to steal your thunder of love.

Remain in your space of love and compassion and keep your heart, not your head. When we "use our heads" we're becoming preoccupied by the circumstances and appearances. Don't think, remain in love.

The only thing I'll die on the sword for these days is when I'm faced with stupidity. Stupidity has always been a hot button for me, but I'm learning to see it for what it really is— no "thing" at all. Let's be clear on the difference between stupidity and ignorance. When somebody is ignorant, they just don't know something. Stupidity is when someone knows better but they choose to be ignorant. It just kills me when I see someone doing something that they know is wrong, yet they continue to do it. I lose it when someone parks in a handicapped zone and says, "I'm only going to be a minute." How disrespectful can a person be? You'd be surprised at how often this occurs in our culture. I've decided that I'll be the handicapped parking police. I'll give the person a "shame on you" sometimes and "scold" them as if they were a child who was about to be grounded. This usually sparks a "confrontation" with the person, so I'm trying to change my tune. I'm choosing love and compassion over lecturing. I'll walk with them into the store. I'll ask a question like, "do you realize you just parked in the only available handicapped spot in the entire parking lot?"

Have you ever noticed how some people need a life-threatening experience to find zest and appreciation for life? Are you growing out of crisis or inspiration? Is yesterday defining who you are? Is yesterday keeping you from right now? Right now is such a precious thing to experience, and focusing your attention on what *has* happened in your life preoccupies you from what *is* happening in your life. Have you ever seen the prime-time news magazines feature a story on someone who experienced a brush with death? No matter the circumstances of the story, the people featured always come away with a clear picture of how precious life truly is. Like it or not, this thing we call life could end in the blink of an eye. Knowing that reality, *why not* make today the greatest day of your life? *Why not* do the one thing you always thinking about but keep putting off? *Why not* tell someone you love them on a daily basis? *Why not* start first by telling yourself that you love yourself? *Why not* have a baby even though you don't think you can afford it? *Why not* experience your right now, *right now?* Stop waiting for your life and start right now! Lose the focus on what *has* happened in your life and move into what *is* happening in your life!

### *Chapter 13 Exercise*
### Set Your Stage for Success!

Before you get out of bed in the morning, solidify your attitude and know that today is going to the best day of your life. Think of all the good things about yourself. Think about the good things you will do in life and how lucky you are to be alive. Don't *ever* let the day tell you how to act, and don't allow yesterday to define who you are today. Leave your perceptions of past experiences and appearances behind. Your life is right now. Embrace it and don't look back. Tie your big toe to the bed post if you need to, but don't get out of bed until you've decided on how *you* want to be.

## 14

# $\mathcal{I}$'m So #@$*% Mad!

## *Stopping anger before it starts*

Anger is like a drug to some people. They have trouble kicking the anger habit. Something happens in their life, they respond with anger. Anger has the detrimental side effects of cigarettes, drugs and alcohol abuse. It affects your thoughts, your words, and your actions. If that wasn't bad enough, anger, along with fear, doubt, and worry actually speed up the aging process. Let's kick anger to the curb where it belongs because it no longer fits into our lives. Anger is a hole of negativity that pulls you out of your conscious bliss when you engage it. "Whatever is begun in anger, ends in shame." – Benjamin Franklin (1706–1790).

To make matters worse, we perpetuate the anger of a bad situation by reliving it over and over. Like some doped-up white mouse in a college lab, we lose ourselves in a maze of negativity. In the end, it's merely a waste of time. Our parents gave us the advice of "Count to ten and breathe." If you haven't listened to your parents lately, you're missing the boat, because that is some of the best advice you'll ever get. It is important for us to recognize that anger is, at its core, merely consuming and counterproductive to our true, authentic self. Reactive anger is mostly an exercise in futility. The person who angers you is obviously stuck in a situation, and what happens when we engage them? We too become stuck. Are you engaging the anger merely to be "right," or are you being led by an authentic purpose? Recognize from this point forward that a need to be "right" or have the last work is nothing more than the call from your ego. Ignore the ego and embrace authenticity. When you embrace the ego and engage anger, it only adds up to more time spent outside of your conscious bliss and love. Why are you engaging at all? Why do you feel the need to enlighten someone who is obviously deep-seated in their anger? Very rarely will anger present itself without the appearance of another person or some other "thing." If the statement, "it takes two to tango" is true, sit this one out. Tell someone who wants to engage your anger, "Sorry, my dance card is full." Ever notice how we've got everyone else's lives worked out but our own? Stop that practice and focus on your life. Nobody needs to be fixed, so concentrate on your life and find your own greatness! Finding your greatness has nothing to do with the engagement of anger.

Sometimes when we get angry, we start to analyze our lives and find other things that anger us. I guess this might be the only positive thing about being pissed off, because a focus is finally obtained. But I believe the whole "pissed off" thing is really just time pissed away. What good does it really do? Again, we're robbed of our position in conscious bliss. Ask yourself: Was anyone hurt? Could I have avoided this? What can be done about it? If your answers were that nobody was hurt, I couldn't have avoided this, and no, there's nothing I can do about it, there's only one thing left to do: *blow it off* and move on. Don't let the problem become more than it is. Don't let it ruin your day. You don't have to ignore your feelings, but don't waste your time being mad. Just think of all that time you could've been in love. Think of all the time you could've been living in joy, bliss, and creativity.

"Would you like me to give you something to cry about?" Remember when your parents asked that one? If it's worth your emotion, then do it, but make sure where the desire to engage is coming from. Unless the desire is authentic to who you are and who you want to become, blow it off. We have enough angry people in the world, so *why not* be the exception? *Why not* become an example of forgiveness, gratitude, and compassion? Take a step back and really see the situation. If needed, get another perspective, another person's point of view, but resist the desire to "react." Find your center and really get to the core of how you feel about the situation. Then, when you're level-headed, tackle the issue. More often than not, you'll find it much easier to deal with anything when you access a positive state of mind. A state of mind that leads with love and compassion is paramount in life. When you move and decide from a point of centeredness and love, the issue that initially made you angry will most likely seem trivial and trite.

*My car was stolen!* Well, be thankful you weren't in the driver's seat when it happened. Who knows—the crazy, misguided gentlemen who took it might've had a gun, and you might've been shot. *I lost my job!* Be thankful, because after the initial reactive panic, you will realize that you never liked the job in the first place. Send your boss a thank-you card. They might've saved you ten years of wasted time in a job that you now realize was time wasted because it wasn't serving your authentic self. *Somebody owes you fifty bucks and isn't returning your calls?* Think of it this way, if this is the type of person they are, it only cost you fifty dollars to get them out of your life. *My girlfriend* or *my boyfriend cheated on me!* This one hurts, but be thankful it happened. Sound crazy? You've been awakened from a sleepwalking life of complacency and surface love. If your lover was capable of doing something like this, do you really think you're meant for one another? Think of all the time you just saved. Things have a way of happening for a reason. Resist the desire to react, and find the blessing.

When the "issue" occurs, we think the world is coming to an end, but we know this to be false. Life goes on; it always has. Life has a way of providing for us, so be open to all possibilities. Remain authentic when faced with the chaos of society's appearances and circumstances.

What about when something really goes bad? Say, for example, someone burglarizes your house. This is a bad situation, but can you find anything good about it? Remember a week before this happened, you were complaining about your desire to live in Oregon, on the edge of a lake, or maybe near the ocean? Who knows—maybe this situation is the universe's way of telling you to act on your dream. You might have never left that comfort zone if the situation hadn't taken place, so be thankful someone took your old stereo and all the other material things you've accumulated. You can always buy a new stereo. The trick here is to see if you can forecast your life and act on things before these drastic situations occur and force your hand. If you had pursued the dream of living in Oregon more seriously, you'd be out of here and the burglary wouldn't have happened in the first place, right? On the other hand, say you already moved to Oregon, living your dream, and your house is *still* burglarized. You'll be surprised how little this causes in reaction, because when we live in the stream of our dreams, circumstances and appearances like this hold little or no value. You recognize material things for what they are. Sometimes if we can't get into gear with our goals and aspirations, the universe will step in and push us over the edge. See if you can eliminate reactive behavior in your life. Don't wait for external circumstances to cause you to act. Act without reaction. This is commonly referred to as pro-action. Be proactive with your goals. Actively think of your dreams and innermost desires. You might not be able to afford the big house on the lake in Oregon, but when you make a move in the direction of your dreams, you know the universe works in your favor. Look to be the catalyst for good things to happen in your life. Be the factor that sets your life in motion. Don't sit around and react to life. Develop a plan and stick to it. Nobody can do it for you. It's up to you. Make that change now! *Why not?*

### Chapter 14 Exercise
### Don't React, Pro-Act!

Are you carrying around any anger in your life? Is someone making you angry? Are you making yourself angry? If the answer is yes, then sit down and ask yourself these three short questions:

1. Could I have avoided this?
2. Is anyone hurt by it?
3. Can I do anything about it?

Once you've gone through this process, either take the steps necessary to solve the problems or move on, but never allow the problem to consume you. If you're experiencing the same types of problems or recurring problems, it's time to wake up. The universe might be trying to tell you something, so look inside and discover why it keeps happening. Reoccurring problems or circumstances can sometimes be disguised as fate showing us the way, so listen and move forward. The point here is to lose reactive behavior all together. Learn how to avoid having your buttons pushed by losing the anger button all together. Exercise the love button in your life by entertaining your authentic emotions through knowing the truth about being you.

## 15

# What Goes Around Comes Around

## *The gifts of giving*

This is a story of what comes around. My office is located on Montana Avenue here in Santa Monica, California. Lined with boutiques, yoga studios, and coffee shops, Montana has become known as the "westside Rodeo Drive." Below the bank of windows that supply my view of the Pacific Ocean is a small parking lot. This parking lot provided me with a new way of "seeing" a few months back.

One morning I noticed a Toyota Camry badly in need of a car wash as it pulled into the parking lot. The car was really dirty. A week later, I saw the Camry again and it still hadn't been washed. A few days after that, I decided to write the owner the following note:

*I dare you to wash your car.*

I had a meeting in Hollywood that afternoon and took the note with me to put on the windshield of the Camry. By the time I got downstairs, the car was gone. I kept the note in my car for the next time I saw it, but more than a week passed without seeing the car, so I finally threw the note away.

I went out of town for ten days on business and on the morning of my return, I saw the Camry pull into the lot. Would you believe it if I told you that the car still hadn't seen a drop of morning dew, let alone a bucket of soapy water? The dirt was like the crust on my Grandma Weldon's pumpkin pie. It had been almost a month since I first noticed the dirty car. A woman quickly jumped out of the traveling pie crust full of scramble. Fumbling to activate the alarm, she dropped her sunglasses. She quickly gathered them up and scurried off to work. I then realized that this woman was living in a world of episodic acute stress. She was five minutes late for her life. I further realized the meaning behind this situation and why it presented itself to my awareness. The appearance of her car didn't bother her at all. The truth of this moment was that the appearance of the dirty car was bothering *me*.

I sat there basking in this moment of awareness, and within five minutes, I was downstairs washing her car. You want to talk about a drive-by car wash? I was in and out of there within eight minutes. I remember laughing the entire time about how crazy this must seem to anyone else. Here I was, washing some woman's car I didn't know. I do remember the feeling it gave me when I did this. I was comforted with a feeling of gratitude for this woman. Without her, I wouldn't have come to this place of awareness of how we're caught by our perceptions and judgments of others. I then reworded the note I wanted to leave a month earlier to read as follows:

*You've just been hit by a random act of kindness. You have seven days to return the favor to somebody you don't know. Peace!*

I wasn't able to see the woman's reaction later in the day, but I know I made her day. I know this act of love caused her to smile. Knowing this causes me to smile on a daily basis. The very next day I was making dinner for a girl friend and we ran out of wine. We walked next door to Fireside Cellars here on Montana Avenue to buy a nice bottle of Cabernet. Inside, we ran into a friend of mine named George. George owns a men's clothing store also located on Montana. George had a friend with him, someone I had never met and they were trying to sell us on a Chilean beer. It was like they owned stock in the beer company, because we got the full-court press. I thanked them for the recommendation, but wine was on our menu. George's friend quickly said, "If you trust me, I'll pick out a really good bottle for you." I thought to myself, "*Why not* see what he comes up with?" As the man escorted us to the row of red wines, he said, "If you really trust me, I'll buy it for you." Without hesitation, I quickly replied, "I really trust you."

The man picked out a nice bottle and proceeded to tell us all about the wine and the vineyard it came from. I loved seeing his excitement in this moment. I could only smile at the sight of his heart. We moved to the counter and George put his bottle of Chilean beer on the counter with our bottle of wine. The total bill came to $68.50! The bottle of beer was maybe four dollars, so that means a man whom I had never met before this moment, bought me a sixty-dollar bottle of wine for no reason. All this a day after I washed a stranger's car. Funny, don't you think? Beautiful, I think. I love that story. I love to become more and more aware of all the love that is in our lives. Giving and receiving love is what life is all about. One of God's many gifts to us is love. I love that.

The truth is, you never know how or when you can affect someone's life with a little bit of kindness. The great thing about the car wash story is that I never saw the car or the woman again. I like to think that it caused some kind of chain of events that made a difference in her life. Maybe, to return the favor of the car wash, she did something nice for someone that ended up getting her a better-paying job. Maybe it caused her to look at the fact that her life had become so routine that she no longer cared about the car she used to love. Who knows? The possibilities are endless, but the fact remains that love was given and received, and our world can only get better when that happens. This is what I know.

Based on the car washing experience, I knew I was onto something. I knew this is how I wanted to live my life, giving and receiving love unconditionally on a daily basis. Then it occurred to me that I already live my life this way, but it was now that I was becoming more conscious of it. Was this my "new way of seeing"? I'm not sure of the reason, but wherever I go, whatever I do, I see love being expressed, and I only want to circulate it to the infinite. I'd much rather live my life in a light of love than in any other light. While I was in college, I came across a list that basically changed the man I would become. The "five most important words" list has been taped to my computer monitor for years and I love it. It reads as follows:

- ✦ The five most important words: *I am proud of you.*

- ✦ The four most important words: *What is your opinion?*

- ✦ The three most important words: *If you please.*

- ✦ The two most important words: *Thank you.*

- ✦ The least important word: *I.*

Wherever it came from it sure is a great reminder for us all. For some reason, probably due to a function of society and the Madison Avenue mentality, some people have made "I" their *most* important word. This is a dangerous trap to enter. Nothing good comes from putting one's self before the grace of others. This is where selfish behavior is born, and we all know the pitfalls of selfish behavior.

One day I was in my car, winding through the hills of Studio City on my way to Universal, when I came across the funniest thing: a woman driving a brand-new luxury car.

Normally this wouldn't be considered funny at all, but the woman was driving on a flat tire as if it wasn't even there. From the looks of the tire, she had been driving on it for some time. The custom-chromed rim was about to be ruined and the cost of a flat tire was about to quadruple if she didn't pull over and take care of the problem. Neglect can be found at the heart of most of our major problems in life. The solution is to pull over and change the metaphoric flat tires of our lives. When we do this, we stop the snowballing effect.

I tried to get the woman's attention as I pulled next to her, but she wouldn't even acknowledge my presence. She was afraid of me because she was trapped by fear. Finally I yelled, "Excuse me, ma'am. Did you know you have a flat tire?" She still wouldn't answer. "Ma'am, you're going to ruin the rim." Finally, she turned and said, "I know about the tire, but I'm almost home." "Where do you live?" I asked. She replied, "At the bottom of the hill." The bottom of the hill was a good mile away. Now it was my mission to convince her that nothing bad was going to happen if she pulled over. This is an example of how drastically our society has deteriorated. Even though she needed help, she was afraid of pulling over. After some reassurance, she finally pulled her limping chariot to the curb.

When I asked her why she was so reluctant to pull over, she said she was afraid of people she didn't know. Hearing her say that just about broke my heart. Here was a woman who, by appearance, could have been my mother. She seemed like a nice lady. Somewhere, somehow, some "thing" caused her to fear the unknown. During the ten minutes it took me to change the tire, she proceeded to open up and share about her life. She asked about my work on *Law & Order*, girl-friends, how long I have lived in Los Angeles, and so forth. She was, as I thought, a very nice woman. She had simply lost hope and was forced off the crowded highway of life. She had chosen to give up. I know we live in a volatile world, but if we lose hope and retreat to our caves, who will lead us? We are the instruments of divinity. It's up to us to make a difference.

As I shut the trunk of her car, my hands black with brake dust, the sweet lady handed me a one hundred dollar bill. I politely declined and informed her that it was my pleasure. She was floored. She didn't understand that I did this without wanting anything in return. Her smile brightened. I like to think that her smile was an indication of her journey back onto the highway of life. This was the roadside assistance she needed to move back into a trusting state of mind. Who knows? I do know that something magical happens when we allow ourselves to open up. When we open ourselves to others, love is expressed. There is a giving and receiving of love. Love found its way back into that woman's heart by way of a flat tire. Lofty thoughts of mine, thinking I made a difference? No. *Why not* think good thoughts like this?

Have you ever heard the story behind the blue ribbon? In 1982, a woman by the name of Helice Bridges designed a small blue ribbon with the phrase "Who I am makes a difference" printed on them. She wanted to make a difference in people's lives by showing them recognition. The movement took off and one day, a New York school teacher gave her class the blue ribbon. She wanted to acknowledge each of them by giving them the ribbons. After the ceremony, she gave everyone two additional ribbons and told them to give them out in the community. One kid gave his ribbon to a junior executive at a nearby company. The junior executive gave it to his boss because he admired his creative spark. The boss went home and gave the second ribbon to his 14-year-old son and told him how much he loved him. The son wept at his father's gesture because he was going to kill himself the next day. He didn't think his father loved him.

Truth is we have no way of knowing what's going on in the lives of others, whether they are complete strangers or intimate friends and family. A simple act of kindness just might have a life-shifting effect on someone. *Why not* go out of your way to make someone's day? "The true measure of a man is how he treats someone who can do him absolutely no good." – Samuel Johnson (1709–1784), author of the first English Dictionary.

### *Chapter 15 Exercise*
## Look to Make a Difference!

You have twenty-four hours to do something nice for someone. Search out opportunities to make a difference in someone's life—someone you don't know. By making a difference in someone's life, you'll make a difference in your own. There is no limit on the expression of love, even for those we do not know.

# 16

## $\mathcal{R}$isk
### *A four-letter word?*

For some reason, the word *risk* has been lumped in with all those "other" four-letter words. Conjuring up negative feelings, risk has gotten a bad rap over the years. If someone hears that risk is involved in a situation, they run for the hills like a jackrabbit. "Always do what you are afraid to do." – Ralph Waldo Emerson (1803–1882).

Much like life, risk-taking comes in all shapes and sizes. At one end of the spectrum, we have the daredevil risk. Usually, this is the skydiving, bungee-jumping risks that are indicative of people who have no fear or an ability to push their fears aside by taking action. They operate without self-doubt and worry. On the other end of the spectrum we have the calculated risk. The people in this category won't move a muscle unless they've considered every possible scenario. If the variables aren't just right, almost perfect, they choose not to move. This is the ultraconservative risk-taker, the kind who feels that if they cover all the variables, they could limit or drastically reduce the probability of failure. When the smoke clears, however, would this even be considered a risk? Sounds more like a calculated business decision to me. Whatever the risk, we're not here to debate which kind is more beneficial. This is about the ability of recognizing the inherent good that comes from risk taking. "You cannot discover new oceans until you have the courage to lose sight of the shore." A wonderful statement and I would love to give credit to the author of it, but it's an anonymous quote. It pierces the very heart of risk-taking. Discovering new oceans doesn't mean going on vacation, either. The dead spots in your life will still be there when you get off the plane, train, or automobile. It's your job to eliminate these dead spots by taking risks through strength, courage and wisdom. By that I mean, you must leave your comfort zone behind, regardless of the fears you might have of the unknown.

"Ya gotta take the good with the bad." Ever hear that one? Complete garbage, so kick it to the curb and forget you ever heard it. Why accept anything that's bad? If there's something bad in our lives, we need to get rid of it—not tomorrow, and not next week, either. Right now is the time for change. Change is for the better. Trust in yourself and make the change for a better life. Make the change for a better you! Why is it that when we find ourselves in a bad situation, we fall into traps of justification? We say "I can't do anything about it now" or "It's not that bad." Those types of statements are toxic to your new style of thinking. Losing them completely from your vocabulary is vital to achieving any goal. Usually someone in a dead-end job or an abusive relationship will use these justifiers to assist in their amnesia. The risk of leaving the comfort zone is too much to handle so they trick themselves into believing a situation isn't the way it actually is. They can't see this way because they are stuck in a chronic state of stress. They aren't willing to *risk* what they have for the pursuit of the unknown. Just because something is familiar, doesn't make it comfortable.

One of the biggest comfort zones, or as I like to call them, unconscious zones, is the zone of relationships. Some people stay in a bad relationship for the sake of being in *any* relationship. They do this because they don't want to risk being alone.

The problem is, this type of behavior robs you of the potential moment of recognizing when your true love enters your life. How do you expect to meet the love of your life when you're in a relationship based on the fear of being alone? Some people jump from one relationship to another without missing a beat. A friend of mine got divorced and within two months, he was already living with another woman. That lasted for a year, and then it was on to the next woman. He dated her for less than three weeks before they moved in with each other. Of course, that ended too. What he's missing is the notion of the individual. There has to be a "me" before there can be a "we." Jumping from one relationship to another because you're afraid of being alone closes the door on divinity. There is a perfect divine order of discovering who you actually are, so if life is leading you down a single life, then there's some reason for it. How do you expect to know yourself when your attention is stuck on the fear of being alone?

One of the greatest quotes from the best-selling book of all time, the Holy Bible, is "Plan for the day, and not the morrow." Jesus Christ broke bread and drank wine that day. He didn't think, let alone worry, about tomorrow; for today, they feasted. We never really know what we're capable of until we make a commitment to excellence. Remember, excellence equates to risk-taking. One of the biggest crimes against ourselves is settling for something we're not passionate about. You have to become a nut for passion—or to say it another way, you have to live a "passion nut" life. Venture around the blind corners of life and live in the land of possibilities. Stand up and fight for your right to be who you want to be. Take a risk and see what happens. Stand in your own light. Don't wait for someone to tell you that it's okay for you to move. Discover your power. You have the power to say what *will* and *won't* happen in your life.

*Chapter 16 Exercise*

## Lose Your Fear by Taking Risks!

Make a list of all your fears. Determine the "who, what, where, when and why" they are based on. The sooner you can become conscious of something that is holding you back, the sooner you can practice eradication and move on. Meet your fears head-on. Begin working on these fears on a daily basis. Mark them off one by one and discover the strength, courage and wisdom you'll have by overcoming them. Do the very thing you are afraid of and discover the power in becoming who it is *you* want to become. Risk the chance of becoming great in whatever it is you dream about.

**Fears I Will Overcome:**

1. _____

2. _____

3. _____

4. _____

5. _____

6. _____

7. _____

# 17

# Success Finds a Way
## *Can it find you?*

"Obstacles are those frightful things you see when you take your eyes off the goal," Henry Ford (1863–1947). Keep your hands on the wheel and your eyes on the road because focus is the key to success. It is vital that you stay true to your vision because persistence will always overcome resistance. You have to see yourself doing the very thing you dream about. Successful people will always find a way to succeed, despite the challenges that lay ahead. The law of accomplishment will always present us with several avenues to choose from when faced with adversity. When some "thing" attempts to divert us from our intended course, we can either, turn around and give up, take a left and go around it, which creates a delay but keeps us on some sort of forward course, or we can move full steam ahead. The "full steam ahead" approach gives you power because you're moving forward with your *intention* without giving up your *attention*. The only thing that can make you give up on your dream is you. Remember that. If you want to give up, you will. If you think about giving up, you will.

When I was a senior in college, I had a full load of classes, a twenty-eight-hour-a-week job, a role in the university play, a girlfriend, and a fraternity-level social life. My time management skills were finally in order, thanks to my father, so I was on track for graduation. I was feeling great about where I was going and what I was doing. About this time of the year, the on-campus senior interviews were taking place. For the marketing department, all the big firms were visiting: IBM, Xerox, Proctor & Gamble, Nabisco, and Hewlett-Packard. Around the last week of the senior interviews, one of my professors asked to see a show of hands from everyone who had taken advantage of the senior interviews. Hands proudly shot up, and a few stories were shared as to what to do and what not to do during the interview process. Then, my professor asked to see a show of hands for those who had yet to participate. I raised my hand.

I looked across the room to see only one other hand raised. My professor didn't bother with this guy named Pete because he never came to class in the first place. I, on the other hand, was an active participant in the class, and often challenged on theoretical issues. "What's the problem, Eric?" he asked. I explained that I wasn't interested in being employed by any of the companies on campus. He quickly jumped into a lecture on the importance of getting comfortable with the interview process. I told him that I didn't need the practice; I was just too busy at this point in my life. Besides, I knew impromptu meetings were a strong point of mine, so I didn't need to go to "practice interviews." I stood my ground and felt good about it. My professor moved in for the kill. "Don't you think you're being a little pompous in your attitude toward these companies?" I told him of my desire to work in the entertainment industry, and meeting with the visiting corporations would only be a waste of time. Needless to say, he wasn't thrilled at my cockiness, and as I look back, I'm sure my delivery was ego-based on top of everything. But it was true—I was actually too busy. I knew what I wanted, and I didn't think I needed the practice.

My professor told me I was being foolish, and suggested that I might have made a mistake by choosing marketing as my major when I should have chosen theater arts or film school. I had heard all of this long before now, so this new "insight" didn't faze me. He walked away with the notion the conversation was over, but it wasn't. I spoke up and reminded him, in the ego-driven "challenge the teacher" tone that I used to have, "Are you teaching me about product placement, timing, problem solving, and everything else involved with marketing a product?" Slowly he turned, like a gunfighter responding to a challenge, and said, "What was that?" I continued, "Why wouldn't marketing be applicable to the entertainment *business?* Isn't a movie just that, a product trying to find a place in a highly competitive and crowded marketplace?" Despite what other people had been telling me, I knew deep down inside that I was on the right track. Should I have challenged him in front of the class like this? Probably not, but when I was younger, I loved the opportunity to question authority. I guess I still do, but now my motivation is born out of respect and genuine curiosity. I was, however, starting to get worried because the year was coming to a close, and I hadn't made a single trip to Los Angeles for a job. Truth be told, I was so bogged down with playing catch-up from all my years of procrastination, I didn't have time.

Graduation was less than a month away, but I kept telling myself not to panic. I was in school for the last seventeen years of my life, what was the sudden rush to find a job? The jobs could wait at least another month, right? I didn't need to dive in right away. I wanted to possibly travel through Europe, or live in Costa Rica for a couple months before getting a job. My mother called a few days later to report her recently moved-in next door neighbor, Christine, was in the television casting business. Mom suggested I bring my resume home during Thanksgiving vacation and talk with Christine. I didn't want to be in the casting business, but I thought, w*hy not?*

After all, I was finally getting an interview with someone in the business. The more I thought about it, the more excited I got.

After Thanksgiving day dinner I went next door to meet with Christine. I'll never forget the moment she opened the door. She was five-foot-seven, with blonde hair and blue eyes, and absolutely beautiful. She was going to be my boss? I remember thinking to myself, have I died and gone to heaven? We had an enjoyable conversation about my plans after graduation, and she informed me that her company was getting ready to do local casting for a Universal Studios television production. The show was a one-hour drama from one of the executive producer's of *Hill Street Blues* and *Miami Vice*. The new show, *Nasty Boys* would air on NBC and star Dennis Franz and Benjamin Bratt. I couldn't hide my excitement and the interview was fantastic. When I graduated, Christine said she would somehow find a place for me within her company. I would be able to live with my mom and pay off some of my student loans *and* work on a network television show? I was indeed going to live my dream.

The phone rang around quarter to five. Christine was calling to tell me that her husband, the line-producer for *Nasty Boys,* had just gotten a call from his personal assistant informing him that she couldn't make the trip to Las Vegas. Christine asked if I would be willing to come over and interview for the job. I think I was knocking on her door before she was able to hang up the phone. I went inside and met her husband, Lynn. Lynn was a veteran TV producer. He drilled me for two hours on hypothetical problems that might occur on the set. I later found out that this type of testing goes on in the Directors Guild of America's assistant director screening program. I remember thinking of my professor's advice on practice interviewing. I sure could've used more practice, but I made my bed, so I had to lie in it.

Lynn offered me the job at the rate of $450 a week. $450 a week? I remember thinking, "I'll be rich in no time." I was in heaven. I was going to work for Universal Studios. Lynn told me production started on December 18. The trip to Europe was off, but that was okay, because I was living my dream. I told him that my last final was on December 17, so I would have no problem being ready. He told me that if I wanted the job, I would need to be back in Vegas no later than December 5. Without even thinking, I said no problem. We shook hands and I ran home to spread the good news. I went back to school. Within two weeks, I finished three written reports, arranged for early final exams, packed up everything I owned and stuffed it into a moving truck. Everything was going as planned, but I had one professor who insisted that I still give my final presentation — in his office. You guessed it, the infamous marketing professor wasn't about to let me off that easy. There would be no room to fudge by padding the audience with tough questions that I would know the answers to. There would be nothing of that sort.

On the Tuesday I was to leave, I spent the morning hours giving my presentation in his office. He gave me some latitude, but still applied the pressure. He was a tough one, but as I look back on it now, I'm thankful for a teacher who actually gave a damn. Isn't it funny how we remember the real tough teachers as we get older? We remember the teacher who challenged us to look deeper into our souls. I received a B– on the presentation, but I managed to pull off an A– for the semester. I was given one of the three A's awarded in his class. I'm still proud of that accomplishment. When I left his class that afternoon, I was filled with the joy of my personal victories. I was the first from the class to land a job, and on that last day in class, some of my fellow students applauded for me. It was such a rush to know that I remained authentic with my dream. Regardless of the skepticism I faced about my choice of majors, I had hung in there and things had a way of working out in my favor.

The *Nasty Boys* job was amazing. I was involved with the day to day production and was on the set every day. I knew this was the beginning of something great. I was living my dream, or so I thought as the other shoe soon dropped. While we were producing our fifth episode of the thirteen-episode order, Universal told the executive producer, Dick Wolf (*Law & Order*), the show was being pulled back to L.A. because the budget was out of control. Thoughts of uncertainty ran through my head. What did this mean for me? Did I still have a job? My boss told me that I was a local hire. A local hire is basically a temporary employee, not a studio employee. When the show moved back to L.A., I would be out of a job.

My dream was in my hand and I wasn't about to let it slip away. During production, I had become friends with the supervising producer, Michael Duggan, who had worked on *Hill Street Blues* and would later become executive producer of *Law & Order*. I asked Michael if there was any way I could come back to L.A. with the show. He told me that they had a full staff in Los Angeles and he didn't know if there was any room. I remember saying, "This is my dream. This is what I want to do." I was out of school and had no commitments to anything else. I was willing to do anything. He said he'd check into it. It was like the circus was leaving town on Saturday morning, and I was a kid who wanted to be part of the high-wire act. It was Friday afternoon, and still no word from Michael. He was staying at the MGM Grand and wasn't answering his phone. I was so bummed out. All sorts of "poor me" thoughts filled my head. Insecurities drove me into a momentary lapse of depression. After "awfulizing" for another hour, I found out Michael was entrenched in a re-write and couldn't answer the phone. He walked in my office that night at six o'clock. I was responsible for sending the scripts to the L.A. script coordinator. Michael told me to be at his office on the Universal lot Monday morning. I eagerly shook his hand and told him I wouldn't let him down.

I packed up my convertible and headed off to Hollywood. This was the start of something special. I could feel it. One of the crew members offered me a spare room in his apartment near the studio until I could find my own place. When I got into town I gave him a call, but he wasn't home. I decided to do some sightseeing. Throughout my journey, I kept checking to see if he was home. Same result. This was an auspicious beginning to say the least. As the sun began to set over the Studio City hills, I started looking for somewhere else to stay. The Universal Sheraton was ninety-five dollars a night! I couldn't afford that, so I kept looking. I finally found a hole in the wall down the street from Universal. The thick, green shag carpet was worn thin in places and the sink in the bathroom was stained with rust. The towels were in desperate need of bleach, but it was thirty-five dollars a night. I could handle these conditions. After all, I was living my dream. I later found out "my friend" took a job in New York and said he forgot about me. Needless to say, we weren't friends very long. I still laugh about that day, however. I remember feeling like Tom Hanks' character in *Big* when he stayed in the hotel all by himself in New York. I was alone, but I was living my dream. I comforted myself with a Fat Burger dinner and a bad TV-dubbed version of *Fast Times at Ridgemont High*. Ironically, the writer of that movie, Cameron Crowe, would later become one of the greatest influences on my career, so I guess it was perfect that his first film was playing on the TV.

The anticipation of my first day at Universal pulled me out of bed at five-thirty. I'll never forget the sunrise as I pulled onto the back lot. A cascade of colors washed over the hills where films like *Psycho* and *Jaws* were shot. It was the moment of the sunrise when I realized this dream of mine was happening. I was hooked. I mean, this is where Hitchcock used to work. This is where Steven Spielberg snuck onto the lot at the age of sixteen years old. I was about to walk where some of my childhood heroes had walked. Yes indeed, I was truly living my dream. It was this dream that would later allow me to sneak onto the sets of *Jurassic Park, Back to the Future, Sneakers,* and *Batman.* I was able to observe some of Hollywood's top directors. Yes, I knew I was in the stream of my dream. I was in the stream for great things to happen.

I soon discovered my job was nothing like the job I held in Las Vegas. There was a well-defined pecking order and I was at the bottom as a production assistant. I was used to going to the set every day and having an active role in the production of the show. At Dick Wolf's office, it would be nothing like I ever imagined. My duties included answering the phones, making photocopies, and all that blah, blah, blah work that goes along with paying your dues. I kept reminding myself that I was living my dream and this was part of the journey. My parents shouldered my frustrations throughout this time. I felt so useless. I was a doer, not a gopher. After two months of this monotonous routine, while I was covering the phones during lunch, I finally approached Dick with a desire to become more involved. He told me, "Relax, kid. You've done the hardest part. You're in. Smell the roses, things will happen." That turned out to be the only advice I ever got from the Wolf man, but it was good advice. I slowly learned ambition is a good thing, but one should never lose sight of what's going on right now.

A few months later, a job opened up in the development department of Wolf Films. I interviewed and got the job. It was a cool job and it satisfied my desire to become more involved, but it was nothing I would make a career out of. It was boring. Truth be told, the boring part was up to me. The boring part was my perspective and opinion of the job. So, I used the time wisely. I soon learned the fastest way out of the trenches was to become a writer. I wanted to become a director, but writing looked like a good way to learn the craft of story-telling. I embarked on a road that would forever change my life. If anyone ever tells you writing is easy, they are sadly mistaken. This was hard work. My heart was leading me so I kept following it. My philosophy was this: if I understand the story process as a writer, it can only make me a better director.

Two years clicked by in the blink of an eye. I still hadn't cracked into the writing rotation of *Law & Order,* but I was learning valuable lessons. I was impatient. I knew I wanted to become a director, and I was rapidly seeing the writing on the wall. It won't happen by sitting behind a development desk. *Law & Order* was shot in New York, so I would either have to move to New York or make a change here in Los Angeles. Disregarding my fear of leaving the company, I gave notice. A few days later, a new producer joined the company with a series commitment from NBC. Robert DeLaurentis was a veteran TV producer who had worked on *St. Elsewhere* and *Alfred Hitchcock Presents.* His new show was called *Mann & Machine* starring Yancy Butler (of TNT's *Witchblade*). I interviewed with Bobby and a week later, I got the job. This was a lateral move in pay, but this wasn't about the money. This was about the opportunity to learn and get myself back on a set. Bobby turned out to be everything in a mentor I needed, professionally and personally. He read all my scripts, no matter how bad they were. He read them and gave me advice on how to improve my writing. Working for him proved to be invaluable. Through his guidance, I began my journey into becoming a man, rooted in authentic desires. I began asking and answering some very tough questions in my life. The calling to become a director was becoming louder and louder, despite the lucrative pay of Universal. I was growing tired of watching other people direct. I wanted to get into the game. I was on the sidelines, but when $1.3 million dollars is on the line each week, it is difficult—if not impossible—to get a shot. You needed to be a member of the Director's Guild of America to direct an episode. How do you become a member? You direct a show that has a contract signed with the DGA. Well buckle my shoe, it's another catch twenty-two.

I did manage to become a Writer's Guild of America member on the show. After *Mann & Machine* got cancelled, I knew it was time to leave behind the comforts and steady pay of Wolf Films to become a full-time writer—director. This was an extremely risky move because hyphenated careers are few and far between. I was looking for more involvement and independency. Fact was, things were moving too slow. I didn't go to college to be stuck answering someone's phones, no matter what the pay was. I left work on July 7, 1996. I was ready to set the world on fire. "Here I am, world, I'm ready! Hello? Can anybody hear me? Is anybody there?" That's exactly how my first year away from Wolf Films was. I filled my bank account with a measly $18,000 from writing residuals. I wondered, "Did I make a huge mistake by leaving behind *Law & Order?*" Thoughts of uncertainty reigned as a full year flew by and I hadn't directed a single thing. Finally, after writing two episodes for USA Networks' *The Big Easy,* I wrote and directed a commercial for The American Lung Association. The commercial was a public service announcement called "Stop the Cycle." Using morphing technology, the commercial displayed a character that morphed from a Hispanic person to Caucasian, Black, and finally Asian. It showed how each culture suffers the same cycle; learning to smoke by watching our elders. Subsequently, I was nominated for a Monitor Award by the International Television Society, which recognizes excellence in television production. My category was "best director in a national commercial." I was up against big-budgeted directors of commercials for Ford, Budweiser, NFL Films, and Coca-Cola. Not bad company for a first-time director. I remember thinking, "Finally, I've arrived." I was sure to set the world on fire now. I would later learn, through time, "arriving" is a misconception. We never really "arrive" in life because life is constantly and forever changing. The only thing that remains constant in this life is who we are. Placing your attention on a preconceived destination is a waste of time. Placing attention upon anything other than your authentic self is a further waste of time. Living in the land of circumstances and appearances of life only snags you away from your greater good. It preoccupies you from your dreams. Be careful of "destination" traps: they are easy to fall into.

I didn't win the Monitor Award, but the amazing thing was everyone wanted to meet the "long shot." In the weeks to follow, I had meetings all over town. I met with Quentin Tarantino's company, A Band Apart. I even met with Propaganda Films, which spawned the career of David Fincher, director of *Seven, Panic Room,* and *Mission Impossible 3*. I met with advertising giants like HKM and Bozell Worldwide. Everyone wanted to meet the guy who slipped into the awards gala with a five-thousand-dollar commercial. Would you like to hear the funny part of this story? Nobody would hire me because I had only done the one commercial. *That,* my friends, is the entertainment business. Everyone said they wanted to keep me on their radar. What am I? A plane stuck in flight, looking for someone's permission to land? I refuse to be a "blip" on anyone's radar.

Frustrated at the prospect of another year going by without capturing my dream, I took the biggest risk of my life. On July 7, 1998, I maxed out twenty-two credit cards and began production on an independent film titled *Kate's Addiction*. Shot in eighteen days, *Kate's Addiction* was financed with $78,000 on credit cards. Out of default, I wrote, directed, produced and executive produced the movie. I didn't have any money for a large crew, so I wore many hats. The pay I was offering to my crew? A measly twenty-five dollars a day. It wasn't a lot of money, but most of them were used to working for free just for the experience. If you ever want to talk about a case study in gorilla film making, let me know. I could go on forever about what "to do" and what "not to do." I had a star that would only work for a few hours, even though we had a contract with her. You see, I signed an "experimental" Screen Actors Guild contract. This meant, any SAG member could halt production if they had an audition for a "real job." If they didn't like the finished product, they could stop me from distributing the film. Basically, I was at their mercy. It was really nerve racking when you show up in the morning with a full day of work ahead of you and the star says she's opening for Smash Mouth on the Santa Monica Pier today. "What time is the gig?" I asked. "Five-thirty, but I have to be out of here at noon." I shot a full day of work before lunch. This was crazy, but I was living my dream and finished the movie in eighteen days.

Having missed the Sundance Film Festival deadline, I submitted a rough cut of *Kate's Addiction* to the Newport Beach Film Festival. They loved it, but in order for them to accept the movie, I would need to finish it for theatrical viewing. This boils down to one thing: money. I needed more money, but my credit cards were maxed-out and I was at a loss. This sure felt like a serious roadblock, but as Henry Ford reminds us, that feeling came from taking my eyes off the goal. It came from being snagged on the problem and not focusing on the solution. I pulled myself out of the funk by calling everyone I knew. I even wrote letters to some of the biggest names in Hollywood asking for help. Nobody responded. I then wrote to the president of the best sound company in the business, Todd-AO. Richard Hassnin responded by dropping my rate to a non-profit level. All we would be responsible for is the labor costs of his employees. Even at this bottom basement price, I couldn't afford it. When you have no money, even the lowest number is too high.

I was at the end of my rope. I had exhausted all connections and the festival was rapidly approaching. If I didn't meet the deadline, it would be physically impossible to finish the film in time. I grew weary of pulling up the boot straps and dusting myself off. I remember sitting on the curb outside of some low-rent sound company feeling totally rejected. I was in the stream of my dream but my self-starting enthusiasm was almost gone. I felt like a long distance runner who was in sight of the finish line, but didn't have the strength to finish. Could this be the end? Did I go through this entire journey only to stall out on the last leg? Orison Swett Marden (1850–1924), the founder of *Success* magazine, once said, "Most of our obstacles would melt away if, instead of cowering before them, we should make up our minds to walk boldly through them." Those thoughts of doubt and giving up didn't fit with me as I refused to give up. I didn't go through all the blood, sweat and tears to cut corners now. I had a vision and I would not compromise. Was I being stubborn? You bet. My last ditch effort before I called my parents was a phone call to a friend in Las Vegas. Bill Brenske was my best friend's uncle and he had been a mentor to both Tommy and me since we were kids in high school. I was out of answers and I needed help.

I explained the situation to Bill and he promised to call me by the end of the day with his answer. After calling his investment partner, Mr. O'Neil, Bill called his wife Lisa for approval. In less than twenty minutes, my cell phone rang. Bill said the money would be in my account by the next morning. In return, Bill, Lisa, and Mr. O'Neil were given participation in the profits of the film. My friends were now my business partners, which added to the pressure, but also the excitement. My internal drive to succeed was fueled now more than ever. I didn't want to let my friends down. I love Bill for stepping in at a time when I thought I was alone. This only further proves that we are never alone, even though sometimes we may feel like it. Bill later informed me that the reason he "dove in" to my dream was because he knew it was from my heart. He knew I was doing something I truly believed in. He was right. Fact is, if you don't have your heart involved, there's no point of even trying.

We had one month to do about three months' worth of work. I had wanted to use the Van Morrison song "Into The Mystic" in the film, but Warner Brothers informed me the song would cost $100,000 for licensing and publishing rights. I tried to explain my passion to the record executive, but her hands were tied. I wanted this song. Some people told me to just find a new song and move on. While shooting *The Big Easy* in New Orleans, I met a musician who was represented by the same lawyer as Van Morrison. How serendipitous this was, now that I look back on it. I wrote a passionate plea to Van through his lawyer, Stan Diamond. I faxed it off and went back to work. The very next day, I received a fax from Mr. Diamond informing me that Van agreed to grant me publishing rights for "Into the Mystic" at no charge. Hear that? No charge. I could use the words and music, but I would need to find someone to cover the song. The solution was a local musician named Michael Lord. Michael has an incredible voice and covered the song beautifully. The licensing situation initially seemed like a roadblock, but I remained in a *full steam ahead* mode. I thought, if I could write to Van, I know he would understand my position. I was doing something against all odds. As an artist, I knew he would respect this and he did.

The "to do" list for my film was a mile long, but we were checking them off one by one. I found a composer, Bill Conn, who had worked with one of the great movie music composers of our time, Hans Zimmer (*Pearl Harbor, Hannibal, Mission Impossible*). At first Bill vacillated about taking the job because of the pay, which was entirely deferred, but he finally agreed to do it because, as he told me, "You've got great enthusiasm, kid." Bill did an amazing job on the score in less than two weeks. Now came time for the mix. Steve Pederson, who received an Academy Award for sound mixing on Ron Howard's movie *Apollo 13*, did my final mix. This was blowing me out of the water. I had set all of this in motion, and the universe was conspiring in my favor to make it happen. Here was an Academy Award winner working on my credit-card movie. Wow. One by one, things fell into their own divine order.

We finally delivered the print to the festival office on the morning the festival was to begin. Worn out from midnight editing sessions and color-timing sessions at four in the morning, we watched as *Kate's Addiction* sold out all screenings. On the final day, I was awarded the festival's Maverick Award, which was given to the "Filmmaker of the Future." *Variety* wrote a blurb on the festival, as did the *Los Angeles Times.* A week later, at a screening in Santa Monica, *Kate's Addiction* was sold to Lions Gate Films for domestic distribution. Two days after that, Saban International bought all foreign territories. We sold the entire world. Hear that? We sold the entire world! As of today, *Kate's Addiction* has made over $2.5 million worldwide for Saban and Lions Gate. I'm currently in negotiations for my next film, *Saltwater Taffy,* a children's adventure movie which I wrote.

Great things can happen if you put yourself in the stream of your dreams. If people looked at the number of films that are made each year and the number of films that actually find distribution, nobody would ever invest in making an independent film. The road is long and full of opportunities. The key is how you perceive the opportunities. It's about how you choose to deal with what's placed in front of you. Some may say that I'm far along on the road of success, but I like to remember that this quest is an ongoing process. It's a journey that never ends. Bottom line: If there's a will, there's a way. Things will happen if you go after what you want. Passion will power you through. Persistence is the key, but make sure your heart is involved. When you're in love with what you do and who you are, nothing else matters. Are you ready to dive into the love waiting to be expressed through and as you? "Never give up, for that is just the place and time that the tide will turn." – Harriet Beecher Stowe (1811–1896), author, *Uncle Tom's Cabin.*

### Chapter 17 Exercise
### Put Yourself in Perspective!

Begin to recognize yourself on a daily basis for what you really are: an amazing, creative, and love-filled individual. No job is too small, no task too trite. There are no small parts in life, only small actors. Whatever you have chosen to do in life, do it with everything you are. Your exercise is to really look at your life and ask the big question: "Am I ready for success? Am I ready to live my dreams? If opportunity presents itself, am I ready to answer the call?" Seek out advice from people who work in your dream stream. Ask them what you could do to better your chances for success. Basically, find a mentor and solicit advice from anyone willing to give it. You'll be surprised at the openness and willingness of others if you look for it. Ask yourself on a daily basis, "What did I do today to make my dream become my reality?" Small steps will turn into long strides.

# 18

# $\mathcal{M}$ost of All
## *Being proud of yourself*

We've talked a lot about spending our time wisely by choosing authentic desires. I'd like to bring our attention to something that is truly a waste of time; external validation over pride for who you are. A lot of the time, we wait for external validation before we become proud of who we are. When you wait and further worry about group acceptance, you're losing sight of the most important element of pride: your own self-pride and acceptance. After all, isn't this the most important element of who we are—being proud of ourselves?

Pride is the direct appreciation of one's self. *Webster's Dictionary* gives the following definition for "pride": *a sense of one's own proper dignity or value; self-respect.* Does this say anything about someone else's opinion? Are you proud of who you are? Do you like and trust yourself? How can we expect to empower ourselves if we don't have some level of self-pride? Truth is, we can't. It's like building a house without a foundation. It doesn't work. Sooner or later, the walls will come crumbling down. As with most things positive and inspiring, love is at the core of pride. Pride is love. Self-assurance is love. Confidence is love. Trust is love. It all boils down to your own self-worth. Is there anything better than self-assurance and love? The purity of "knowing" that we are truly great is vital if we are to become what we "see" for ourselves. Without self-assurance and pride, we become an empty vessel floating through the rivers of life. Success doesn't mean anything without pride. Financial success without pride is a bank account. Nothing more.

It is one thing to be proud of yourself right now, but are you proud of who it is you are becoming? The person you are becoming has nothing to do with material trimmings. Material accumulation has nothing to do with pride. There is no price tag on pride and success. Media and excessive propaganda has brainwashed us into thinking that if you aren't driving a German luxury car and living in the posh neighborhoods of some zip code, you're nothing. I once heard an interview with a rap music mogul who commented on the financial rewards of popular music: "After your third Rolls Royce, it's still just a car." How many trips around the world does someone have to take before they realize happiness and fulfillment starts at home? Home is where the heart is. Or better yet, heart is where the home is. If you aren't happy at the core of who you are, it doesn't matter where you travel because you will always be there. Money can't buy happiness. Happiness starts and ends with you.

Basically, everything in your life starts and ends with you. Money is a by-product of your dreams. Think about the woman who works in a nonprofit center for battered women. Would you consider her less than successful because she drives an older car? Would you consider her less than successful because she lives in an apartment in an unfashionable neighborhood in an undesirable zip code? I'll bet her life is more fulfilling than most of the luxury-car-driving CEO workaholics of the world. Why? She's following the true master of all drives — her heart. Are you following your heart, or are you snagged by thoughts of accumulation? Are you following your heart, or are you following your ego?

I remember the moment I became aware of the many

pitfalls that can occur when we measure success by material accumulation. I was home for the holidays and a friend of mine confessed to me that envied my life. Envied me? How was this possible? He's got a big house, a beautiful wife, a luxury-car-filled garage, the respect of his peers, and a weekend hobby of flying airplanes. What could possibly make him envious of my life as a struggling artist, living in a rent-controlled apartment here in Santa Monica? He's got everything a man could want, right? Driven by materialism in his early years, he was now recognizing the effects of serving the money master—an unfulfilled soul. You see, he was making money, and that was it. His marriage was taking a nose dive, and he began to dive into the escapism of alcohol. Was the lack of love for his job carrying over into his marriage? Whoever said "Misery begets misery," was right. It's hard to come home from a job you despise and then be Mr. Happy-Go-Lucky with your wife and children. My friend began to question just about everything in his life. This situation was such an eye opening experience for me. Before this moment, I was snagged by thoughts of failure because I was challenged by my finances. This was a misconception of mine and I'm sure I'm not alone with it. Material accumulation has nothing to do with your love. Your love and life come from within. Remember your vibratory frequency? Where's your light coming from? Externally, or internally?

Together, my friend and I concluded the main ingredient lacking in his life was passion. His job was a "good-paying job," but it didn't bring him the excitement he so desired. He confessed he never liked the job. The thing he liked most was the pay. Though he had all the trimmings of success, he had a life without passion. We talked about his dreams. We talked about the little kid inside of him that used to call out, "When I grow up, I want to be a _____." After college, he was lured in by ego-stroking statements like "You'll be making this much money per year, and we'll give you a company car." Corporations have long been known for luring college graduates with material rewards. Why? Because we're taught that "making a good living" is the only thing that matters after you leave college. He soon discovered that once they get their hooks in you and you grow accustomed to this new lifestyle, it's that much harder to leave it behind. You become dependent on the lifestyle, and the debt you've accumulated doesn't allow you the freedom to leave. Before you know it, you're stuck in a job and you begin to wonder, "How did this happen?" The key is to make a life and not a lifestyle. Material success had become a price tag for my friend.

Six months after we talked, my friend called to inform me that he was selling the house and filing for a divorce. On top of that, he quit his lucrative job to become a full-time airline pilot. He said he kept hearing a question that I asked him during our discussion: "What do you love to do?" He realized that being up in a plane was the answer. At first, he said he thought he was being silly, but *why not* love what you do for a living? I could hear the conviction in his voice when he talked about these new decisions. At first I was a bit concerned by his complete stripping of his life, but he said he knew he was on the right track when his wife was only worried about the financial impact of his changing jobs. She couldn't see past the "cut-backs" they might have to incur. He knew the road was going to be challenging, but it didn't matter. This was something he always thought about but never had the courage to go after, because it wasn't a "conventional job." He came to visit a few months ago, and you could see the happiness pouring out of him. You could see it in his eyes. You could see it in his actions. You could feel he was in the grips of clarity for the first time in his adult life. He was in love with his life again, but most of all he was proud of his decision. He was proud of himself for having the courage to step out of his status quo. He was proud of what he was doing with his life because he was following his dreams.

In college I'll admit I was drawn in by the power and material benefits of success. I often wondered what it would be like to fly up to San Francisco for a morning business meeting. To this day, I still wonder what it would be like to have an expense account. If there was one kind of job that I was always good at, it was sales. I could sell sunglasses to a June bug in the dead of winter. When I had a job selling advertising for a small local paper, I thought I had found my calling. It came so easy to me. I dreamed of big meetings and the company car. I became so organized that it got a little scary at times. Then, one day, something occurred to me as I was on my way to rehearsal for the Shakespeare play, *All's Well That Ends Well.* I remember feeling truly excited about the rehearsal. I felt a power that one can only feel by doing something they absolutely love. This love didn't happen overnight, mind you. This is a love that was born out of practice. It was at this moment I knew somehow, someway I wanted to be involved with the entertainment business.

I will admit, I do have thoughts of owning my own house, barbecuing in my own backyard, but right here, right now I'm happy. The backyard won't define who I am. The backyard is a "thing," and as we know, no "thing" can bring about happiness. The fruition of one's passion is more powerful than any bank account can ever be. I'd be a completely different person if I had gone into the advertising business. I did what worked for me. It may not work for the next guy, but this path works for me, and I'm embracing it.

One of the main thrusts behind self-pride is accomplishing your goals. Whether the goal is of great proportions or something small, the important thing is that we trust in ourselves enough to move in the direction of our dreams. It's this high level of trust in ourselves that is the main element of the new behavior model we're creating. We are constantly shaping this model from the day we are born. This new behavior model is vital to the new style of thinking we want for ourselves. It's time to break out and find our passions. Go after what you want in life and be proud of yourself. Take pride in who you are because you're moving in the direction of your dreams. There is nothing more powerful than that. Remember what Winston Churchill (1874–1965) said: "Never, never give up." You can do it. I can do it. We can do it together.

## Chapter 18 Exercise

### Establish Your Road Map!

Do you know where you're going? Have you asked yourself lately? Does your journey elicit a feeling tone of love and compassion? Your exercise is to write down a set of goals that move you into the direction of your dreams. The only rule here is that you *must* commit to something for each of the seven goals. Dream big, dream tall, and never consider yourself as being small. The answers to life are found through love. Are you loving your life?

1. Weekly goal (shortest term):

   _____

   _____

2. One-month goal (shorter term):

   _____

   _____

3. Three-month goal (short term):

_____

_____

4. One-year goal (middle term):

_____

_____

5. Three-year goal (long term):

_____

_____

6. Five-year goal (longer term):

_____

_____

7. Ten-year goal (longest term) :

_____

_____

Once you have determined a goal (of whatever time period) you must further break it down into workable steps. For example, if you were planning a trip to Europe next year, you would have a laundry list of "things to do" before you left. You would need to set an exact date for departure, buy an airline ticket, obtain a passport, choose a durable suitcase or backpack, pick a destination, etc. Each of the items listed in this example are steps which need to be completed before you reach your goal of being in Europe in one year. Goal setting is like planning a journey—you have to consider every step to get there. By breaking the final goal into workable steps, you can see exactly what you need to do by marking off each step as you go. Remember, leaps and bounds are comprised of smaller, more manageable steps.

### *Departing Wish:*

Well, here it is; we've come to the end of the book, but this is by no means the end. This is the beginning of the life you dream of. This is the beginning of the *you* that *you* desire. My wish is that you become everything you dream and you dream everything you become. I am in deep gratitude for the time you've invested in this desire to become your dreams. My heart smiles knowing you've made it through. I hope it's been as informative for you to read as it has been for me to write. Good luck and most importantly, have fun! Call your mother. Remember, a smile goes a long way in your life and in the lives of others. Dive in, your life is waiting. *Why not* get the most out of who you are? *Why not* get the most out of who you want to become? Simply put, *Why not.*

# Acknowledgments

As I begin to write these very words of thanks, humility and divine gratitude are mine. The love dives so deep here. You are the warm blanket for two on a cold winter's night. The tender smile a mother reserves for her child. The sound of raindrops dancing you awake, knowing you have three hours to sleep. Everything is different now. A one-way doorway has been given me. I move forward as my heart leads me. My passion forever serves me. Oh my God, can it be this wonderful? Can it really be this good? The gentle answer is: yes it can. When we look at life through a kaleidoscope of love, we soon realize it is ours to have: the life *and* the love. Question remains: how many different ways can we see it? My heart continues—searching for that answer. Imagine the difference. Imagine the possibilities. Simply, imagine. All things are possible through love.

**THE BLOCK OF LOVE & THANKS:** God, Mom, Dad & Sharon, Garret & Jill, Stacey & Craig, Riley, Tyler, Carley, Mathew, Grandma & Grandpa Weldon, Aunt Eva, Ike & Harris, Grandma & Grandpa Koelsch, Grandma & Grandpa DelaBarre, Uncle Wally & Aunt Edie, Uncle Alan & Aunt Connie, Aunt Joanne, Brian & Amy, Stacey & Jeff, Dr. Michael Beckwith, Rickie B.B. and my Agape family, Mark Victor Hansen, Trudy, Jimmy & Chelisa, Matt, Tommy, Terry, Jack, Jobe, Welch, Roy, Zip & Di, The D's, The Brenskes, Mr. O'Neil, Dale, Simon, Dewayne, P-Lee, Panaro, Nova, Lopez, Caser, June Boyce, Cindy Benson, Cameron Crowe, P.T. Anderson, Hoblit, Hitchcock, Spielberg, Lucas, Warshaw, Tom & Marianne, Gio, Palmer, Tubbs, JC, Fordes, Leon, Ursittis, Lachs, Tom, Stephen, Alli, Bryan, Daisy, Noelty & D, The Goldbergs, Fredo & D, Diamond, Junior, Memo, Jaz, Chester, Nicole Dorsey, Author Power and my dear friend, Michelle. I thank you all for your friendships, inspirations, love and support. Life wouldn't be the same without you.

# Works Cited/Permissions

Eternal Dance Records, *I Release and I Let Go.* Words and music by Dr. Rickie Byars-Beckwith and Dr. Michael Beckwith.

Canfield, Jack. *Chicken Soup for the Soul* series. Andrews McMeel Publishing, 1993.

Cole-Whittaker, Terry. *What You Think Is None of My Business.* Jove Publishing, 1991.

Hansen, Mark Victor. *Chicken Soup for the Soul* series. Andrews McMeel Publishing, 1993.

Kersey, Cynthia, *Unstoppable,* Source Books, 2000.

Be Fit Enterprises, Jack & Elaine LaLanne.

*Star Wars: Expisode V — The Empire Strikes Back.* Reference courtesy of Lucas Film LTD™. All rights reserved. Used under authorization.

Peck, Dr. M. Scott. *The Road Less Traveled.* Simon & Schuster, 1980.

*Zig Ziglar Training Systems.* 2002 Chenault Drive, Suite #100, Carrollton, TX 75006

# Bibliography/Research

Famous Quotations Network. www.famous-quotations.com

Fitzhenry, Robert I. *Barnes & Noble Book of Quotations.*
Harper Perennial—A division of Harper Collins
Publishers. 1987

Fraga, Naomi, 2000. *The Function and Mechanism of Bio-*
*luminescence* www.anabaena.net/bio/bio.html

Frank, T.M. & Case, J.F., 1988. *Visual spectral sensitivities*
*of bioluminescent deep=sea crustaceans,* Biol. Bull., 175,
261-273

Gage, J. D., and Tyler, P., 1992. *Deep-sea Ecology: A Natural*
*History of Organisms at the Deep-Sea Floor.* Cambridge
University Press, Cambridge, 503 pp.

Naval Meteorology and Oceanography Command website:
www.pao.cnmoc.navy.mil

Oceanography and Bioluminescence:
www.oceanlink.island.net

Webster's Online Dictionary: www.dictionary.com

Search Engines: www.google.com   www.hotbot.com
www.yahoo.com

# Order Form

Telephone/fax orders: Call (877) 595-6996

Email orders: seven@sevenpublishing.com

Postal orders:  Seven Publishing
Sales Department
P.O. Box 1123
Santa Monica, CA  90406-1123

Website sales:  www.sevenpublishing.com
www.amazon.com

Please send FREE information on (check all that apply)
❑ Speaking/Seminars    ❑ Consulting/Life coaching
❑ Mailing lists

❑ Please send me _____ copies of *Why Not* at $14.95 each.

Name _____

Address _____

City _____

State _____ Zip _____

Telephone _____

Email _____

*Sales tax:*  Please add 8.25% for products shipped to California addresses.

*Shipping by air:*  United States: $5.00 for first book
$2.00 for each additional product (estimate).
International: $10.00 for first book
$5.00 for each additional product (estimate).

*Payment:*        ❑ Check   ❑ Money order
Credit card:    ❑ Visa      ❑ MasterCard   ❑ American Express
Card number _____ Exp. _____
Name on card  _____

*"Have I told you today...?"*